THE ARMY LISTS OF THE ROUNDHEADS

AND CAVALIERS.

THE ARMY LISTS
OF THE
ROUNDHEADS AND CAVALIERS,

CONTAINING THE NAMES OF THE OFFICERS IN THE ROYAL AND PARLIAMENTARY ARMIES OF 1642

EDITED BY
EDWARD PEACOCK, F.S.A.

Cover shows the Battle of Marston Moor, 2 July 1644

The Naval & Military Press Ltd

published in association with

FIREPOWER
The Royal Artillery Museum
Woolwich

Published by
The Naval & Military Press Ltd
Unit 10 Ridgewood Industrial Park,
Uckfield, East Sussex,
TN22 5QE England
Tel: +44 (0) 1825 749494
Fax: +44 (0) 1825 765701
www.naval-military-press.com

in association with

FIREPOWER
The Royal Artillery Museum, Woolwich
www.firepower.org.uk

In reprinting in facsimile from the original, any imperfections are inevitably reproduced and the quality may fall short of modern type and cartographic standards.

PREFACE.

HOSE who have ſtudied that period of our annals which is occupied by the reign of Charles the Firſt and the Commonwealth, not only in the pages of modern hiſtorians and of contemporaries who wrote conſciouſly for poſterity, but alſo in the immenſe maſſes of unclaſſified and often uncatalogued documents, journals, ſtate papers, letters, treatiſes, ballads, and ſermons, in which the hopes, fears, and deſires of the people expreſſed themſelves from day to day, may probably have remarked, if their purſuits have led them to contraſt our Civil War with other portions of Britiſh or European hiſtory, that then, for the firſt time in the modern world, individual perſonality began to exerciſe a marked effect upon contemporary politics. In the preceding ages, from the time indeed when freedom ſunk under the organized imperialiſm of the Cæſars, until the outburſt of modern thought in the ſixteenth century, human progreſs had been but little accelerated by perſonal qualities. The ignorance of external nature was too denſe, the all-pervading influence of the dominant theology too ſtrong, the terrors it wielded and the puniſhments it threatened too frightful for the energy of any one perſon to become conſpicuous in directing public events or moulding the thoughts of others, except

b

in thofe rare cafes where the minds of men had already been prepared by the Church's teaching, or by their inherent or inherited fuperftitions. In the career of St. Bernard indeed, and the few others of his ftamp, who fhed fuch luftre over the dark times in which they were placed, we fee the religious inftinct of Weftern Chriftendom ftirred to a higher pitch of devotion by the labours of a fingle man; but where the leffons of the reformer took a direction contrary to ecclefiaftical teaching (and then theology feemed to embrace the whole area of human thought), one refult only was poffible. The fate of thofe who ftruggled to win freedom for themfelves and their kind is a fufficient proof that it was neither the want of intellect, energy, nor high-fouled devotion, that rendered their lives and labours unfruitful. Even the paffionate prophecy and withering fcorn of the great Florentine could do nothing towards roufing mankind from its lethargy. The firft defire of his heart was indeed accomplifhed; Dante won for his Beatrice the higheft place in the ideal world of love and beauty, but againft the "fhe-wolf" even the invectives of the "Inferno" were powerlefs.

The education of the European mind has progreffed flowly; it was not until the Tudor period of our hiftory that fociety could have exifted without the protection of a powerful religious cafte. A univerfal theocracy was the only inftitution ftrong and free enough to curb the oppreffor, and with a fufficiently extended mental vifion to attempt the work of legiflation : by its means the brutal tyranny of the feudal lord was fomewhat kept in check; and his fiercer paffions, at leaft, did not pafs entirely without rebuke. Laws were made for the protection of flaves, infants, and *women*, fuch as even a Norman baron or an Italian count feared to difobey. It does not feem poffible that moral truths could have been brought home to the hearts of the people by any other means. If fo great

[*PREFACE.*]

a misfortune could have happened as the premature overthrow of this spiritual dominion it is almost certain that a similar institution, or once differing in outward accidents only, would have taken its place. And if it had not been so, the people would have lapsed into mere pagan sensualism; a compound of Teutonic materialism and Southern creature-worship without the nobleness of the one or the poetry of the other.

The great religious contests of the sixteenth century, while they released the races of Northern Europe from subjection to one class of ideas which they had outgrown, left almost everything to be accomplished in the direction of personal freedom. It is doubtful whether any of those engaged on either side in that memorable strife even understood what is now meant by liberty.

The singularly complex nature of our political and social relations on the accession of the Stuart dynasty tended greatly to develope individual energies, and thus to produce that marked contrast between the Civil-War era and all preceding ones, which is perhaps the most interesting phenomenon presented by that memorable contest. Probably no descendant of the Plantagenets, then alive, was more unfitted to rule England than the weak person whom political necessity forced upon us on the death of the noble-minded Elizabeth. It would have taxed the highest energies of a wise and brave sovereign to have governed a land so distracted with religious factions with dignity and in peace. James possessed neither courage nor wisdom, but had the absence of those virtues been his chief defect, his reign might have caused less evil. His political bigotry, mitigated as it was in action by his extreme cowardice, was not calculated to produce the worst results; but unfortunately, like many other feeble-minded men, he took intense delight in theological speculation. As the head of the established religion in England it was the obvious duty of the chief magistrate to make that body as little offensive to the people as the nature of so singular a compromise would admit of; but, from influences which it probably would be easy to trace to their origin, the king's mind was bent upon pursuing an opposite course. The extreme nature of the religious factions into which his realms were divided, spurred on the zeal of the theologian not to be a minister of peace but an enforcer of uniformity. The Catholics, who had received in the early part of the reign some slight mercy, when the monarch found himself sufficiently powerful to do so, were persecuted with unrelenting severity. The increasing body of Puritans (a designation which must be understood to include persons of nearly all varieties of opinion who were opposed to despotism in the state and extreme Episcopalian views on Church government) hated the ruling powers almost as intensely as did their brethren of the Roman obedience, and with nearly as good reason; for, although they were not subject to capital punishment, like the religious teachers of the ancient faith, their lives were rendered miserable by state tyranny. The Puritans certainly had not, at first, any strong feelings against monarchical power when restrained within due bounds,—some, indeed, professing to the last their desire for "a covenanted King," but they naturally became, as time wore on, less and less attached to the existing order of things. It is probable that a strong-willed and unprincipled monarch might have played off these factions against each other with considerable personal advantage. It is evident that James endeavoured to do so, and as he had at times able ministers about him, it is not unlikely that even he might have succeeded had England been his only kingdom; Scotland and Ireland happily presented unsurmountable obstacles to the crushing out of either of these religious bodies. The northern kingdom was entirely Puritan; the Catholic Church in that region had not merely fallen,--- its members had been so hunted down by their successors, that hardly an avowed professor of the old religion was to be found. Episcopacy, indeed, was still supposed to exist, but its strange and unedifying history was so well known, that we cannot suppose it appealed very forcibly to the consciences of any but those dependent on government patronage. On the other hand, Ireland had clung with the tenacity of despair to the mediæval form of Christianity—it was the only thing that connected her with the far-off past, that carried back the memories of her poor persecuted children to times when they had at least one powerful protector on earth from the oppression of their conquerors. This passionate attachment decked the mythic past with the rainbow tints of unreal beauty, it became part of an Irishman's faith that his country had once had a golden age of peace, prosperity, and virtue, under the mild guardianship of the Church of God.

The attempts made to convert these kingdoms to the king's views were too weak to produce any effect except irritation; but they must be borne in mind in calculating the forces which produced the revolution that followed.

Charles was a far nobler man than his father: had he ruled in other times he might have left a favourable impression on posterity; in the circumstances in which he was placed his higher qualities were almost entirely hidden. Whether it was by force of hereditary transmission, or the result of education, that Charles resembled James cannot now be known, but the same weak nature is remarkable in the child as in the parent,—the same obstinacy, the same theological instincts with even less distrust of his own power of enforcing conviction, and a greater affection for the mechanical parts of religious worship. His faith in the sanctity of his own office was probably more sincere than his father's. It was dangerous in proportion to its sincerity.

The history of the political and religious struggles of these

[PREFACE.]

reigns, of the forty years' battle for liberty, fought with varying fuccefs at Weſtminſter when there was a parliament at the Council Board, in the law-courts and the ſhires when the king ruled alone, has come down to us in a very unattractive form. The various leaders have as yet had but little juſtice done to their memories, the more obſcure men have quite paſſed out of mind. Let us remember that to them we owe much of what followed both of good and evil.

The long conteſt, ere an appeal to arms was thought of, prepared Engliſh minds for ſelf-government, and ſhook to its baſe that belief in the holineſs of the kingly office which the Reformation had foſtered, and which ſubſequent events had developed into an article of faith. Ere the war of words was ſuſpended by a ſterner conflict, I believe that among the maſs of the people the dream of the divine right of kings had paſſed away for ever. A figment ſuch as that, once ſhattered, could never be reſtored; even the *ſaturnalia* of the Reſtoration could only reproduce its ſemblance in thoſe profeſſionally intereſted. The cry—

"Cæſar in urbe ſuâ Deus eſt,"

found no echo in men's hearts. If the reader wiſhes to hear it, and is not to be deterred by blaſphemy or filth, let him read the ſermons of the court-preachers and the rhyme-books of the court-poets.

It is not my intention, in this reprint of a Civil-War tract, to trace, even in the mereſt ſkeleton manner, the hiſtory of the period. A word or two ſeems, however, to be required to account for the appearance of this little book. I have long been making collections relative to the lives of thoſe perſons who were engaged on both ſides during the Great Civil War. In the work I have in progreſs I ſhall include, as far as poſſible, every officer who bore a commission from King or Parliament, and many other persons who rendered themselves conspicuous in the convulsions of the time. Of course I shall not omit to give a place to the many noble women also who suffered on either side. It will be readily understood, that although the work in question will be made as concise as is possible, consistently with communicating the facts of the various lives, it is yet a laborious undertaking, which cannot be brought to a conclusion for some years. It was, however, suggested to me by my publisher, that a reprint of the following Army List would be welcomed by many students as a handy work or reference in reading contemporary historians. Its usefulness to those engaged in topographical and genealogical studies is evident. To such a book it was perhaps unnecessary to add notes; I have, nevertheless, for the convenience of the general reader, given a line or two of biographical memoranda to the names of most of those persons who rendered themselves prominent. To have enlarged them further so as to include the more obscure would have been but to anticipate very imperfectly a future publication. The tract, of which the following pages are a reprint, is preserved in the Bodleian Library. I never saw another copy, but I believe one or two more exist; it is, however, of extreme rarity. The list of the Earl of Essex's army is to be found also in a separate pamphlet, with which this edition has been compared. A reprint of its title-page occurs here in the proper place.

Although the date 1642 occurs on the title, it is certain that this List was not issued until that year had, according to modern computation, closed. It will be borne in mind, however, that the legal year in the seventeenth century began on the 25th of March, the feast of the Annunciation of the Blessed Virgin Mary, and that, therefore, a book issued from the press before that day in the year 1643 would bear the date of the previous year. The occurrence of Philip Skippon, as "Serjeant Major Generall and Prefident of the Councell of Warre," is decifive on this point.* It is not fo eafy to account for the name of "Sir Faithful Fortefcue" being retained in the lift of the Parliamentary army.

My efpecial thanks are due to Monfieur J. A. Van Lennep of Zeyft, near Utrecht, for a long and extremely interefting communication relative to Dr. Doreflaus, which I have ufed in the note attached to that perfon's name. I have a melancholy pleafure alfo in expreffing my obligations to the late Rev. John Ward, of Wath Rectory, near Ripon.

E. P.

Bottesford Manor, Brigg,
    December 15, 1862.

NOTE.

To this Second Edition I have added an Appendix, confifting of four other lifts of foldiers, which will be found ufeful by ftudents of feventeenth-century hiftory. The notes alfo have been revifed and added to, and fome errors corrected.

I have received valuable information from Colonel Chefter, the Rev. Edward Saint Leger, and William H. Turner, Efq.

The Index is mainly the work of my daughters, Florence and Mabel.

Bottesford Manor, Brigg,
    Aug. 12, 1874.

---

* Clarendon's *Hiftory of the Rebellion*, royal 8vo. 1843, p. 382.

A CATALOGUE

OF THE NAMES OF

THE DUKES, MARQUESSES,

EARLES and LORDS, that have abſented themſelves from the Parliament, and are now with His Majeſty. And of the Names of the Lords that Subſcribed to levie Horſe to aſſiſt his Majeſtie with A Copie of all the Cavaliers of his Majeſties Marching Army with the number of Captaines in each ſeverall Regiment; every Regiment containing a thouſand Souldiers.

As alſo, a liſt of the Army of his excellency, Robert Earle of Eſſex: With the names of the Troops of Horſe under the Command of William Earle of Bedford. Each Troop conſiſting of ſixtie Horſe; beſides two Trumpetters, three Corporalls, a Sadler, and a Farrier. With the Inſtructions ſent by the Parliament to his Excellency.

A liſt of the Navie Royall, and Merchant Ships: the Names of the Captaines and Lievtenants; their men and burdens for the Guard of the Narrow-ſeas, and for Ireland.

Moreover, the Names of Orthodox Divines, preſented by the Knights and Burgeſſes as fit perſons to be conſulted with by the Parliament touching the Reformation of Church Government and Liturgie.

Laſtly The Field Officers choſen for the Iriſh Expedition, for the Regiments of 5000 Foote and 500 Horſe.

PRINTED 1642.

A CATALOGUE OF THE NAMES OF
THE DUKES, MARQUESSES, EARLES AND LORDES, THAT HAVE ABSENTED THEMSELVES FROM THE PARLIAMENT, AND ARE NOW WITH HIS MAJESTIE.

The Lord Keeper.[1]   Marqueſſe of Hertford.[3]
Duke of Richmōd.[2]   Marqueſſe Hamilton.[4]

---

[1] Edward Lyttelton, ſon and heir of Sir Edward Lyttelton, of Henley, co. Salop, Knt. Born, 1589; educated at Chriſt Church, Oxford; M.A. 1609; D.C.L. 1642; Recorder of London; Solicitor General, Oct. 17, 1634; knighted June 6, 1635; Chief Juſtice, Jan. 27, 1639; Lord Keeper of the Great Seal, Jan. 23, 1640; created Baron Lyttelton, of Mounſlow, co. Salop, Feb. 18, 1640; joined King Charles I. at York, 1642; a Privy Counſellor and Colonel of a foot regiment at Oxford. Died at Oxford, Aug. 27, 1645; buried in Chriſt Church—Wood's *Athenæ Oxon. ſub nom.* Lloyd's *Memoires*, p. 582. Nicholas's *Hiſtoric Peerage*, 1857.

[2] James Stuart, ſecond Earl of March in the peerage of England, and third Duke of Lenox in Scotland. Created Duke of Richmond, Aug. 8, 1641; K.G. Died, 1655. He was one of the four noblemen who were permitted to be preſent at "their maſter's burial."—*Life of Clarendon*, 1843, p. 1049.

[3] William Seymour, created Marqueſs of Hertford, June 3, 1640. Reſtored to the title of Duke of Somerſet, 1660; K. G. Died, 1660. He alſo was one of the four peers who witneſſed the burial of Charles I.

[4] James Hamilton, Marqueſs and afterwards Duke of Hamilton in the peerage of Scotland; ſecond Earl of Cambridge in the peerage of England. Beheaded by the Commonwealth, March 9, 1649.

4 [ARMY LIST.]

Earle of Cumberland.[5]	Earle of Devonſhire.[11]
Earle of Bathe.[6]	Earle of Carlile.[12]
Earle of Southampton.[7]	Earle of Clare.[13]
Earle of Dorſet.[8]	Earle of Weſtmorland.[14]
Earle of Saliſbury.[9]	Earle of Monmouth.[15]
Earle of Northampton.[10]	Earle of Lindſey.[16]

---

[5] Henry Clifford, fifth Earl. Died, 1643.

[6] Henry Bourchier, fifth Earl. Died, 1654. "A great ſcholar .... always aſſerting the king's intereſt, attending him in his counſel in York, and his general in his affairs in the Weſt, till being taken priſoner, 1642, when he was rendered uncapable of ſerving his king and kingdom, he grew weary of the world, paying for his loyalty 900*l.*"—LLOYD's *Memoires*, p. 650.

" They took priſoner the Earl of Bath in Devonſhire, who neither had, or ever meant to do the king the leaſt ſervice; but only out of the moroſity of his own nature, had before, in the houſe, expreſſed himſelf not of their mind."—CLARENDON's *Hiſt.* 1843, p. 297.

[7] Thomas Wriotheſley, fourth Earl of Southampton. Succeeded as ſecond Earl of Chicheſter, 1653. Died, 1667. He was one of the four noblemen who were preſent at the funeral of King Charles I. Created K. G. at the Reſtoration."—CLARENDON's *Life*, p. 1049.

[8] Edward Sackville, fourth Earl. Killed Lord Bruce in a duel beneath the walls of Antwerp, 1613. Died, "17th of July, 1652, and had ſepulture with his anceſtors at Withiam."—COLLINS's *Peerage*, 1735, vol. i. p. 443.

[9] William Cecil, ſecond Earl. K. G. Died, 1668.

[10] Spenſer Compton, ſecond Earl, "was born at Compton, in Warwick-ſhire, the very ſame day and hour that the Powder Traytors were defeated at Dunchurch, in that County."—LLOYD's *Memoires*, p. 353. Slain at Hopton Heath, co. Stafford, March 19, 1643; buried in All Hallows Church, Derby.

[11] William Cavendiſh, third Earl. Died, 1684.

[12] James Hay, ſecond Earl. Died, 1660.

[13] John Holles, ſecond Earl. Died, 1665.

[14] Mildmay Fane, ſecond Earl. Died, February 12, 1665; buried at Apethorp, co. Northampton.

[15] Henry Carey, ſecond Earl. Died, 1661.

[16] Robert Bertie, tenth Baron Willoughby de Ereſby. Created Earl of Lindſey, Nov. 22, 1626; Lord Great Chamberlain; K. G.; Lord High Admiral, 1636; Governor of Berwick, 1639; General of the King's forces at the breaking out of the civil war. Mortally wounded at the battle of Edge Hill, Oct. 23, 1642, aged 60 years; buried at Edenham, co. Lincoln.—ALLEN's *Hiſt. of Lincolnſhire*, vol. ii. p. 295   *Gent. Mag.* 1808, p. 18.

[*CHARLES I.*]

Earle of Newcaſtle.[17]
Earle of Dover.[18]
Earle of Carnarvan.[19]
Earle of Newport.[20]

Earle of Thanet.[21]
Lord Moubray.[22]
Lord Strange.[23]
Lord Willoughby.[24]

"At Edgehill that was true of him and his Countreymen, the Loyal Gentry of Lincolnſhire, that was obſerved of Cataline and his followers: That they covered the ſame place with their Corpſes when dead; where they ſtood in Fight, whilſt living."—LLOYD's *Memoires*, p. 314.

[17] William Cavendiſh. Created Earl of Newcaſtle, March 7, 1628; Duke of Newcaſtle, 1664. K.G. Died, 1676.

[18] Henry Carey, fourth Baron Hundſon. Created Earl of Dover, March 8, 1628. Died, 1668.

[19] Robert Dormer, ſecond Baron Dormer. Created Earl of Carnarvon, Aug. 2, 1628. Slain at the firſt battle of Newbury, Sept. 20, 1643. His jewels and plate were ſeized by the Parliamentary army while on their way to Oxford. He was run through the body by a trooper to whom he was perſonally known. When aſked if he had any ſuit to make to the king ere he paſſed away, the dying cavalier replied:—"I will not die with a ſuit in my mouth to any king ſave to the King of Heaven."

[20] Montjoy Blount. Created Earl of Newport, in the Iſle of Wight, Aug. 3, 1628. Died, 1665.

[21] John Tufton, ſecond Earl. Died, 1664.

[22] Henry Frederick Howard, ſon and heir of Thomas Howard, Earl of Arundel. Summoned to the Houſe of Peers during his father's life, April 13, 1639, as Baron Mowbray. He ſucceeded to his father's earldom in 1646.

[23] James Stanley, ſon and heir of William Stanley, Earl of Derby. Summoned to the Houſe of Peers during his father's life; ſucceeded to his father's earldom in 1642. He was defeated at the Battle of Wigan-Lane, co. Lancaſter, by Col. Robert Lilburne, but ſucceeded in joining King Charles II. at Worceſter, after whoſe rout there, Sept. 3, 1651, he fled with him into Staffordſhire. Taken priſoner at Newport, in Cheſhire, by Colonel Edge, tried by court martial, and beheaded at Bolton, in Lancaſhire, October 15, 1651. The timber of the ſcaffold on which he ſuffered is ſaid to have been a relic from Lathom Houſe.

[24] Montague Bertie, ſon and heir of Robert Bertie, Earl of Lindſey; ſummoned to Parliament during his father's life as Baron Willoughby; K.G; Lord Great Chamberlain. Died, 1666. Commanded the Royal Guards at Edge Hill. He was one of the four peers who ſaw the body of King Charles buried at Windſor, and endeavoured, ineffectually, to diſcover its reſting-place after the Reſtoration.

[*ARMY LIST.*]

Lord Longavill.²⁵
Lord Rich.²⁶
Lord Andover.²⁷
Lord Faulkconbridge.²⁸
Lord Lovelace.²⁹
Lord Paulet.³⁰

Lord Newarke.³¹
Lord Coventry.³²
Lord Savill.³³
Lord Dunfmore.³⁴
Lord Seymor.³⁵
Lord Capell.³⁶

---

²⁵ Charles Longueville, fon and heir of Sir Michael Longueville and Sufan Gray, his wife, fifter of Henry Gray, eleventh Baron Gray of Ruthin, and eighth Earl of Kent. Claimed and was allowed the Barony of Gray in 1640. He is called Lord Longueville to diftinguifh him from his contemporary, Sir Thomas Gray, called Lord Gray of Grouby, the fon and heir of Henry Gray, fecond Baron Gray of Grouby, who was created Earl of Stamford, co. Lincoln, 1628, and from William Gray, firft Lord Gray of Werke.—NICHOLAS' *Hiftoric Peerage*, 1857.
Lord Gray of Ruthin died, at Oxford, of fmall-pox, June 7, 1643; buried in All Hallows Church.—DUGDALE's *Diary, edited by Hamper, fub die*.

²⁶ Robert Rich, fon and heir of Robert Rich, fecond Earl of Warwick. Succeeded to the Earldom of Warwick, 1658. Died, 1659.

²⁷ Charles Howard, fon and heir of Thomas Howard, firft Earl of Berkfhire. Summoned to Parliament in the life of his father, as Baron Howard of Charlton; fucceeded to his father's Earldom, 1669. Died 1679.

²⁸ Sir Thomas Belafyfe, Bart. firft Lord Fauconberg of Yarm, co. York. Created Vifcount Fauconberg of Henknowle, co. Durham, Jan. 31, 1643. Died, 1652.

²⁹ John Lovelace, fecond Baron. Died, 1670.

³⁰ John Poulett, firft Baron Poulett of Hinton St. George, co. Somerfet. Died, 1649.

³¹ Henry Pierrepoint, fon and heir of Robert Pierrepoint, the firft Vifcount, who was created Earl of Kingfton-upon-Hull, July 25, 1628; and was flain in action, July 30, 1643, during his paffage in a pinnace from Gainfborough to Hull as a prifoner of War. Henry Pierrepoint died in 1680.

³² Thomas Coventry, fecond Baron Coventry of Aylefborough, co. Worcefter. Died, 1661.

³³ Thomas Savile, fecond Baron. Created Vifcount Savile, in the peerage of Ireland, 1628; Earl of Suffex, 1644. Died, 1671.

³⁴ Sir Francis Leigh. Created Baron Dunfmore of Dunfmore, co. Warwick, 1628. Earl of Chichefter, 1644. Died, 1653.

³⁵ Francis Seymour, firft Baron Seymour of Trowbridge, co. Wilts. Died, 1664.

³⁶ Arthur Capel. Created Baron Capel of Hadham, co. Hertford, Aug. 6,

[*CHARLES I.*]

A CATALOGUE OF THE NAMES OF THE LORDS THAT SUBSCRIBED TO LEVIE HORSE TO ASSIST HIS MAJESTIE.

TO pay horſes for three Moneths, thirty dayes to the Moneth, at two ſhillings ſix pence *per diem*, ſtill advancing a Months pay, the firſt payment to begin ſo ſoone as the King ſhall call for it after the Commiſſions ſhall be iſſued under the Great Seale. In this Number are not to be reckoned the Horſes of the Subſcribers, or thoſe that ſhall attend them.

	Horſe.
The Prince	200
The Duke of Yorke	120
Lord Keeper	40
Duke of Richmond	100
Lord Marqueſſe Hertford	60
Lord Great Chamberlaine [37]	30

1641. Beheaded by the Commonwealth for defending Colcheſter, March 9, 1649; buried at Hadham, co. Hertford. His arms were Gules, a lion rampant between three croſſlets fitchée, or. In alluſion to which, after his death, this diſtich became current:—

> "Our Lion-like Capel undaunted ſtood
> Beſet with croſſes in a ſea of blood."

There is a "pleaſant ſtory" in Clarendon concerning Lord Capel's miſſion from King Charles I. to the Earl of Kingſton to borrow money, which gives an amuſing picture of the times.

[37] Robert Bertie, tenth Baron Willoughby de Ereſby and Earl of Lindſey. See Note 16.

[ARMY LIST.]

Earle of Cumberland	50
Earle of Huntington[38]	20
Earle of Bath	50
Earle of Southampton	60
Earle of Dorſet	60
Earle of Northampton	40
Earle of Devonſhire	60
Earle of Dover	25
Earle of Cambridge	60
Earle of Briſtoll[39]	60
Earle of Weſtmerland	20
E. of Barkſhire and L. Andover[40]	30
Earle of Monmouth	30
Earle Rivers[41]	30
Earle of Carnarvan	20
Earle of Newport	50
Lord Mowbray	50
Lord Willoughby	30

---

[38] Henry Haſtings, fifth Earl. Steward of the Duchy of Lancaſter, and Lord Lieutenant of the counties of Leiceſter and Rutland. Died, Nov. 1643.

[39] John Digby. Created Earl of Briſtol, Sept. 15, 1622. Ambaſſador extraordinary to Spain to negotiate the contemplated marriage of Prince Charles with the Infanta; interceded with James I. for indulgence to Roman Catholics. A commiſſioner to treat with the Scots at Ripon, 1640. Among the propoſitions tendered by the Lords and Commons to the King in 1643, the ſixth was:—'That the Earl of Briſtol may be removed from your majeſty's councils."—CLARENDON's *Hiſt.* p. 338. Died, 1653.

[40] Thomas Howard, firſt Baron Howard of Charlton and Viſcount Andover. Created Earl of Berkſhire, Feb. 7, 1626; K.G. A commiſſioner to treat with the Scots at Ripon, 1640. " The government of that hopeful and excellent Prince [afterwards Charles II.] was committed to the Earl of Berkſhire for no other reaſon but becauſe he had a mind to it, and his importunity was troubleſome."—CLARENDON's *Hiſt.* p. 455. Died, 1669.

[41] John Savage, ſecond Earl. Died, 1654.

[*CHARLES I.*]

Lord Gray of Ruthin [42]	10
Lord Lovelace	40
Lord Paget [43]	30
Lord Faulconbridge to come	
Lord Rich	30
Lord Pawlet	40
Lord Newarke	30
Lord Mountague [44]	30
Lord Coventrey	100
Lord Savill	50
Lord Mohun [45]	20
Lord Dunfmore	40
Lord Seymor	20
Lord Capell	100
Lord Faulkland [46]	20
Mafter Comptroller [47]	20
Mafter Secretary Nicholas [48]	20

---

[42] See Note 25.

[43] William Paget, fifth Baron. Died 19th October, 1678. Buried at Drayton, co. Middlefex. He was the perfon who read in the Houfe of Lords the charges of the Scotch Commiffioners againft Archbifhop Laud, 1640.—OLDMIXON's *Hiftory of the Stuarts*, p. 159.

[44] Edward Montagu. Created Baron Montagu of Boughton, co. Northampton, 29 June, 1621. When upwards of eighty years of age he was committed to the Tower by the Parliament, where he died, 1644.

[45] Sir John Mohun, Bart. Created Baron Mohun of Okehampton, co. Devon, 15 April, 1628. Died, 1644.

[46] Lucius Carey, Vifcount Falkland of Falkland, co. Fife, in the Peerage of Scotland. Slain at the Battle of Newbury, 19th September, 1643.

[47] Sir Peter Wych. Had been ambaffador to Conftantinople, from whence he returned but a fhort time before the breaking out of the Civil War. Clarendon fays he was "a very honeft plain man." He died at Oxford, 5th December, 1643, and was buried in Chrift Church Cathedral.—DUGDALE's *Diary, fub die*. Arms, azure, a pile ermine.

[48] Edward Nicholas. Made Secretary of State after Secretary Windebank fled abroad, 1640.

Lord Chiefe Juftice Banks[49] 20
The Lord Thanet is not here but one hath undertaken
for 100 for him

          Sum. totall. 1695.

COPY of a Lift of all the Cavaliers of his Majefties Marching Army, with the number of Captaines in each feverall Regiment, and every Regiment containing about a thoufand Souldiers.

Imprimis 1 Regiment.

The Earle of Newcaftle Lord Generall of His Majefties foot Forces.	Captaine Hemings.
	Captaine Acton.
	Captaine Gyles.
Lievtenant Colonell Rich.	Captaine Fifher.
Sergeant Major Babthorpe.	Captaine Andrewes.[51]
Captaine Fleetwood.[50]	Captaine Froft.
Captaine Waters.	

---

[49] Sir John Banks, born at Kefwick. Knighted, 1ft Auguft, 1634. One of the Privy Council at Oxford, where he died, 28th December, 1644. Buried in Chrift Church. See his epitaph in Wood's *Hiftory of Oxford*. Sir John Banks was the hufband of the gallant lady who defended Corfe Caftle.

[50] William Fleetwood, afterwards a colonel in the Royal Army. Son of Sir William Fleetwood of Aldwinkle, co. Northampton, cupbearer to James I. and Charles I., and Comptroller of Woodftock Park. He was half brother to George Fleetwood and Charles Fleetwood the Parliamentary officers. Arms, parted per pale, nebule azure and or, fix martlets counter-changed.

[51] Eufebius Andrews was fecretary to Lord Capel, educated for the Law, withdrew from the Royal Army, 1645. Tried by a Court of High Commiffion and beheaded for high treafon againft the Commonwealth, 1650.

[*CHARLES I.*]

2 Regiment.

Collonell Lord Taffe an Irishman.[52]	Captaine White.
	Captaine Hill.
Lievtenant Colonell Sir John Rodes.	Captaine Farryer.
	Captaine Whiteacre.
Serjeant Major, Thomas Treveere.	Captaine Floyd.
	Captaine Douglas.
Captaine Upton.	Captaine Winter.
Captaine Hobbey.	

3 Regiment.

Collonell Haftings.[53]	Captaine Venner.
Liev. Collonell Langley.	Captaine Hodges.
Sergeant Major Stanley.	Captaine Johnfon.
Captaine Fryer.	Captaine Fifher.

4 Regiment.

Collonell Sir Thomas Glenham.[54]	Liev. Collonell Vaughan.[55]

---

[52] Theobald Taffe, fon and heir of John, firft Vifcount Taffe, in the Peerage of Ireland.

[53] Second fon of Henry, fifth Earl of Huntingdon, who died 14th November, 1643, by Elizabeth, third daughter of Ferdinando Stanley, Earl of Derby. Created Baron of Loughborough, co. Leicefter, 23rd October, 1643. Died without iffue, 1666.

[54] Sir Thomas Glenham was fucceffively Governor of York (furrendered, July 16, 1644), Carlifle (furrendered, June 28, 1645), and Oxford (furrendered, June 20, 1646). Confined by the Parliament in the Fleet prifon. Died in Holland before the Reftoration.

"'Tho. Glenham cui caftra Carleolente
& Eboracenfe Monumentum funt
& Oxonium Epitaphium."—Lloyd's *Memoires*, p. 552.

His brother, Henry Glenham, fome time Dean of Briftol, was Bifhop of St. Afaph, 1667–1670.

[55] It is probable that Sir George Vaughan of Penbrey is the perfon here

Sergeant Major Wagftaffe.⁵⁶ | Captaine Starkeley.
Captaine Long. | Captaine Smart.
Captaine Coney.⁵⁷ | Captaine Jackfon.

5 Regiment.

Collonell, Sir Francis Wortley.⁵⁸ | Lievtenant Collonell Ruffell.

---

indicated. He was feverely, but not fatally, wounded by a blow on the head with a pole-axe at Lanfdowne fight, July 5, 1643. Another perfon of this name, Sir William Vaughan, fought for the King in South Wales, Chefhire, and Shropfhire. He was killed near Dublin, Aug. 22, 1649.

⁵⁶ Sir Jofeph Wagftaffe was wounded when the Royalifts took Lichfield, 1643. Engaged in the Weftern rifing, 1655, and was with difficulty difuaded by his companions from hanging the Parliamentary Judges and the High Sheriff of the county, who had fallen into their hands at Salifbury. After the ruin of the enterprife he efcaped abroad.—Clarendon's *Hiftory*, p. 825.

⁵⁷ The Coneys were a Lincolnfhire family, feveral of whofe members were engaged on the Royal fide during the Civil War. I am unable to identify the perfon mentioned above with any certainty. Sir Sutton Coney, fon and heir of Sir William Coney, Knight, compounded for his eftate in the fum of 2648*l*. A Captain Coney is ftated to have been flain *ex parte regis* at Whalley, in Lancafhire. A William Coney was one of the Lincolnfhire gentlemen who offered to fubfcribe horfes for the King in the fummer of 1642. A Richard Coney of Grantham was indicted for High Treafon at Grantham Seffions in the fpring of 1643, by the adherents of the Parliament. A man defcribed as "Captaine Corney," but who I believe to be the perfon who ferved under Sir Thomas Glenham, was taken prifoner by Oliver Cromwell at Burleigh Houfe, and fent in cuftody to Cambridge, in July, 1643. The Elizabethan Heralds fay that the firft of the Coneys who fettled in England came from "Byam," in France, with Ifabella, wife of Edward II. There is a pedigree of the family in the Lincolnfhire Herald's Vifitation of 1562. Arms, fable, a bar and two barrulets between three conies current, argent. MS. F. 22. *Queen's Coll. Oxf.* fol. 38. Yorke's *Union of Honour, 2nd*, pages 28. *Tanner MS.* LXII. I. fol. 196. *Decl. of Commons upon two letters fent by Sir John Brookes.* Dring, 24. *Mr. Charles Dallifon, his Speech*, fol. 1642 (Soc. Ant. Broadfides). *Royal Martyrs*, fol. 1660.

⁵⁸ Sir Francis Wortley was fon of Sir Richard Wortley, Knight, of Wortley, co. York. Educated at Magdalen College, Oxford, created a Baronet, June 29, 1611. In the early part of the Civil War he fortified

[*CHARLES I.*] 13

Serjeant Major Waller. | Captaine Stafford.
Captaine Tukes. | Captaine Shelton.⁵⁹

6 REGIMENT.

Lord Grandifon, Lievtenant Generall.⁶⁰ | Serjeant Major Willoughby.
Liev. Collonell John Digby.⁶¹ | Captaine Tempeft.⁶²
 | Captaine Morgan.

Wortley Hall for the King. He was taken prifoner at Walton Hall near Wakefield, the feat of the knightly family of Waterton, on the 3rd of June, 1644. Authorities differ as to the time and place of his death; it is, however, certain that he departed to his reft before the monarchy was reftored. He was the author of feveral books, a lift of which may be feen in Wood's *Athenæ Oxon*. His arms were argent, on a bend between fix martlets gules, three bezants. Motto, Τας φιλιας σπουδαζω, τας εχθρας καταφρονω.—HUNTER's *Deanery of Doncafter*, vol. ii. pp. 308-326.

⁵⁹ Serjeant Major Sheldon was mortally wounded at Lanfdowne fight, July 5, 1643, by the explofion of an ammunition-waggon.—CLARENDON's *Hift*. p. 404.

⁶⁰ William Villiers, Vifcount Grandifon in the peerage of Ireland, fon and heir of Sir Edward Villiers, Prefident of Munfter; brother to George Villiers, Duke of Buckingham, by his wife Barbara, daughter of Sir John St. John of Tregofe, co. Wilts, and niece to Oliver St. John, created Vifcount Grandifon, with limitation of the title to his niece's pofterity. Lord Grandifon was wounded at the fiege of Briftol, July 26, 1643, and died of his wounds at Oxford the 29th of September following. He lies buried under a ftately monument in Chrift Church Cathedral, which his daughter, Barbara Villiers, afterwards Duchefs of Cleveland, erected to his memory.

⁶¹ Sir John Digby, a younger fon of the Earl of Briftol (note 39). Raifed a troop of horfe for the King; commanded the cavalry at the battle of Stratton, May 16, 1643. He was one of the fix perfons excepted from mercy at the furrender of Pontefract Caftle, but fucceeded in eluding his enemies by lying hid within its precincts for about ten days, and then making his efcape unobferved. Sir John Digby furvived the Reftoration. —CLARENDON's *Hift*. pp. 397, 425, 670. SURTEES' *Mifcellany*, vol. i. pp. 2, 93.

⁶² John Tempeft, ninth fon of Sir Stephen Tempeft of . . . . co. York. Slain at the taking of Drogheda, Aug. 14, 1649. He was a Roman Catholic. Arms, argent, a bend between fix martlets, fable.—DUGDALE's *Herald's Vifit. Yorks.* 1665-6, p. 360.

14   [ARMY LIST.]

Captaine Crane.⁶³
Captaine Musgrave.
Captaine Badger.

Captaine Hillyard.⁶⁴
Captaine Muggridge.

7 Regiment.

Collonell Endimion Porter.⁶⁵
Lievtenant Collonell Vavasor.⁶⁶
Sergeant Major Stanhope.⁶⁷

Captaine Williams.
Captaine Berry.
Captaine Tisdale.

---

⁶³ The House of Commons resolved on 10th Dec. 1642, that Sir John Spilman, Knight, Sir William Doyly, Captain Crane, and other persons of the county of Norfolk, should be "forthwith sent for as delinquents for affronting the committees when they were met upon the service of the Parliament." John Crane of Longhton, co. Bucks, was fined 1080*l.* on 23rd Sep. 1647; his offence being "that he deserted his dwelling and lived in Oxford" when it was a royal garrison—*Com. Jour.* II. 884; V. 313.

⁶⁴ Robert Hillyard of Beverley and of Winestead, co. York, son of Sir Christopher Hillyard, Knight. Created a Baronet after the Restoration. Arms, azure, three mullets, or.—Poulson's *Holderness*, vol. ii. p. 473.

⁶⁵ Gentleman of the bedchamber to Charles I. One of those who accompanied him, when Prince of Wales, to Spain. Died abroad before the Restoration.

⁶⁶ Three brothers of the family of Vavasour of Haselwood, co. York, were in the King's service. They are thus noticed in Dugdale's Pedigree (*Herald's Visit. co. York*, 1665-6, p. 345):—

"I. Sir Walter Vavasour of Haselwood, Bart. Colonell of a Regiment of Horse under the right honorable Willm Marquesse of Newcastle, for the service of K. Charles the first, in the times of the late Rebellion. Æt. 53 ann. 13 Aug. 1666.

"II. Willm Vavasour a Major in that Regimt of Horse under his brother.

"III. Thomas Vavasour slayne in yᵉ Battaile of Marston Moore neer Yorke, fighting on the behalfe of K. Ch. the first, aº 1644."

⁶⁷ Philip Stanhope, first Baron Stanhope of Shelford, and Earl of Chesterfield, had two sons in the Royal Army.

Ferdinando, his fourth son, M.P. for Tamworth in the Parliament of 1640; D.CL. Oxford, 1642. Slain at Bridgford, co. Notts, 1643. This is probably the person here indicated.

Philip, fifth son, lost his life at his father's seat at Shelford when it was taken by storm, Oct. 27, 1645.

[*CHARLES I.*] 15

Captaine White.
Captaine Owen.[68]

Captaine Beefley.
Captaine Thirlow.

8 REGIMENT.

Colonell Afhburnham.[69]
Lievtenant Bruerton.
Sergeant Major Carey.[70]
Captaine Huet.
Captaine Fowler.

Captaine Ridgley.
Captaine Wafher.
Captaine Bowen.
Captaine Ballard.[71]
Captaine Weeks.

9 REGIMENT.

Colonell Bellafis.[72]
Lievtenant Collonell Murrey.
Serjeant Major Pope.
Captaine Holloway.

Captaine Legge.[73]
Captaine Withers.
Captaine Hodges.
Captaine Homer.

---

[68] Sir John Owen of Klinenney, co. Caernarvon. Vice-Admiral of North Wales; wounded at the taking of Briftol, July 26, 1643. Tried by the High Court of Juftice with the Duke of Hamilton and Lord Capel, fentenced to death, but fubfequently pardoned.

[69] William Afhburnham, fon of Sir John Afhburnham of Afhburnham, co. Effex, and brother to John Afhburnham who was one of the Royal Commiffioners for the treaty of Uxbridge. He was a member of the Parliament of 1640. Governor of Weymouth, which he furrendered, and occupied Portland Caftle, June 14, 1644. After the Reftoration made Cofferer to Charles II. Died without iffue, 1679.

[70] Sir Henry Carey of Cockerington, co. Devon, Knight.

[71] "Sir Thomas Middleton, and Colonel Mitton, took a garrifon of the Kings near Mountgomery, and in it, Colonell Ballard the governor."— WHITELOCK, Dec. 1644. Slain at the fiege of Taunton, co. Somerfet.— *Micro-Chronicon*, 1647.

[72] John Belafyfe, fecond fon of Thomas, firft Vifcount Falconberg (fee note 28). Created Baron Belafyfe of Worlaby, co. Lincoln, Jan. 27, 1645. Wounded at the taking of Briftol, 1643. Defeated and taken prifoner at Selby, co. York, April 11, 1644. Governor of Newark, Oct. 20, 1645, which he furrendered by command of the King, May, 1646. Imprifoned upon fufpicion of defigning new troubles, April 16, 1651. Liberated, Nov. 2, 1659. Died, 1689.

[73] William Legge, wounded at Lichfield, April 8, 1643. Imprifoned

Captaine Metoo,
Captaine Barret.
Commiffary Wilmot, Mufter-Mafter Generall, one Troop of Horfe.[74]

Secretary Nicholas, Secretary of State, one Troope of Horfe.
Mafter Sidenham, Knight Marfhall, one Troope of Horfe.

10 REGIMENT.

Vifcount Killmurrey, Sergeant Major Generall.[75]

Liev. Colonell Sir Faithfull Fortefcue.[76]

---

while Governor of Oxford, Sept. 17, 1645, owing to his friendfhip with Prince Rupert, whofe commiffion the King had taken from him.

[74] Henry Wilmot, fecond Baron Wilmot in Ireland. Created Baron Wilmot of Adderbury, co. Oxford, June 29, 1643, and Earl of Rochefter, Dec. 13, 1652. He had ferved in the Low Country Wars before the beginning of the domeftic troubles. Appointed Commiffary-General of the Horfe in the expedition into Scotland. Taken prifoner by the Scotch at the battle of Newburn, Aug. 28, 1640. Reftored by the Commiffioners who met at the treaty of Ripon, September, 1640. Wounded at the battle near Worcefter, Sept. 23, 1642. Defeated Sir William Waller at Roundway Down, July 5, 1643. Arrefted by the King for high treafon, 1644. Accompanied Charles II. to Scotland, 1650. Died, 1659.

[75] Robert Needham of Shenton, co. Salop, fecond Vifcount Needham in the Peerage of Ireland. Died 1653, and was fucceeded, as third Vifcount, by his fon Robert, who joined in the rifing in favour of Charles II., Auguft, 1659. In "a lift of the prifoners of Quality now fecured in Chefter," publifhed in the *Mercurius Politicus, Sept.* 1–8, 1659, occur "Lord Kilmorey" and "Mr. Thomas Nedham, Brother to Lord Kilmorey."

[76] Sir Faithful Fortefcue was fecond fon of John Fortefcue of Buckland Filleigh, co. Devon, and Sufannah, daughter of Sir John Chichefter of Rawleigh. He married, *circa* 1604, Anne, daughter of Gerard, firft Vifcount Moore. By this lady he had ten fons and fix daughters. His fecond wife was Eleanor Symonds, a widow, by whom he had no iffue. At the Reftoration he was made a Gentleman of the Privy Chamber. He was colonel of the third troop of horfe raifed for the expedition into Ireland, 1642, and with his troop was draughted into the Parliamentary Army under the command of the Earl of Effex. At Edge Hill battle, Sir Faithful Fortefcue with his whole troop left the Parliamentary Army "and prefented himfelf and his troop to Prince Rupert . . . . The fudden and unexpected revolt of Sir Faithful Fortefcue with a whole troop . . . . had

[CHARLES I.]

Sergeant Major Pollard.[77]
Captaine Bulhead.
Captaine Prowfe.
Captaine Thomas.

Captaine Colesfoote.
Captaine Atkinfon.
Captaine Bateman.
Captaine Denby.

11 Regiment.

Sir Lewis Dives, Colonell.[78]
Liev. Colonel Lucy.
Sergeant Major Withrington.[79]
Captaine Browne.

Captaine Thomas Furbufh.
Captaine Ley.
Captaine Johnfon.
Captaine Slingfby.[80]

12 Regiment.

Colonell Sir Charles Lucas.[81] | Liev. Colonell Stanley.

---

not fo good fortune as they deferved; for by the negligence of not throwing away their orange-tawney fcarfs, which they all wore as the Earl of Effex's colours, and being immediately engaged in the charge, many of them, not fewer than feventeen or eighteen, were fuddenly killed by thofe to whom they had joined themfelves."—CLARENDON's *Rebellion*, pp. 308, 309.

Arms, azure, a bend engrailed, argent, cotized, or.

[77] Sir Hugh Pollard, flain at Dartmouth, Jan. 18, 1646.

[78] Wounded at Worcefter, Sept. 23, 1642. Made prifoner at the taking of Sherborne Caftle, of which he was governor, Aug. 15, 1645. Efcaped from cuftody, Jan. 30, 1649.

[79] Sir William Widdrington, firft Baronet. Created Baron Widdrington of Blankney, co. Lincoln, Nov. 10, 1643. " He was one of the firft who raifed both horfe and foot at his own charge, and ferved eminently with them under the Earl of Newcaftle."—CLARENDON's *Hift*. p. 763. Mortally wounded at the battle of Wigan Lane, 25th Aug. 1651. CARY, *Mem.* ii. p. 341.

[80] Sir Henry Slingfby, Bart. of Scriven, co. York. A member of the Parliament of 1640. Defeated by Sir Hugh Cholmley at Guifborough, Jan. 16, 1643. Taken prifoner in Cornwall, Jan. 1650. Imprifoned in Pendennis and Exeter Caftles. Tried by a Court of High Commiffion. Beheaded on Tower Hill, June 8, 1658. An interefting diary, written by Sir Henry Slingfby, has been preferved and twice printed. The beft edition is that edited by D. Parfons, M.A. 8vo. 1836.

[81] Sir Charles Lucas, elder brother (born of the fame parents, but before wedlock) of John, firft Baron Lucas of Shenfield, co. Effex, and

Sergeant Major Kelley. | Captaine Burley.
Captaine Hodges. | Captaine Strangewayes.
Captaine Ford. | Captaine Whiteaway.

13 REGIMENT.

Colonell Sir George Gotherick. | Captaine Johnſon.
Lievtenant Colonell Waſhington. | Captaine Lever.
| Captaine Burrówes.
Sergeant Major Powell. | Captaine Sutton.
Captaine Iſaack. |

14 REGIMENT.

Colonell Oſborne.[82] | Captaine Holyday.
Liev. Colonell Savage. | Captaine Huſſey.
Sergeant Major Oneale.[83] | Captaine Buttler.
Captaine Forſter. | Captaine Jones.
Captaine Vaux. | Captaine Fidler.

---

next heir of his brother's Barony and eſtates.—NICHOLAS's *Hiſtoric Peerage*, 1857, p. 301.

Tried by Court Martial and ſhot after the ſiege of Colcheſter, Aug. 28, 1648. "He was very brave in his perſon, and in a day of battle a gallant man to look upon and follow ; but at all other times and places of a nature not to be lived with, of an ill underſtanding, of a rough and proud nature, which made him during the time of their being in Colcheſter more intollerable than the ſiege."—CLARENDON's *Hiſt.* pp. 664, 5.

[82] Edward Oſborne of Kiveton, co. Notts, Knight. Created a baronet, July 13, 1620. Vice-Preſident of the North of England, 1629. Father of Thomas Oſborne, firſt Duke of Leeds.—THORESBY's *Ducatus Leodienſis*, p. 2.

[83] Daniel O'Neill was active in oppoſition to the Earl of Strafford. Committed to the Tower by the Parliament, from whence he eſcaped in women's clothing, and fled to the Low Countries. He returned and joined the King at the breaking out of the Civil War. After the Reſtoration, Charles II. let him the poſt-office to farm. Died, 1664. He was the only Proteſtant of his family. "It is more to be called an Oneal than an Emperor in Ireland."—LLOYD's *Memoires*, p. 665.

[*CHARLES I.*]

Prince Robert, Generall of the Horſe.
Sir Thomas Byron,[84] chiefe Commander of the Princes Troopee containing about 500 Horſe.
The Earle of Briſtoll, two Troops.
The Earle of Crawford,[85] three Troops.
The Lord Digby,[86] two Troops.
Lord Capell, two Troops.
The Lord Willoughby, two Troops.

The Lord Grandiſon,
Lord Kilmurrey,
Lord Rich,
Sir Charles Lucas,
Sir George Gothericke,
Sir Francis Wortley,
  each of them a Troop of Horſe; Beſides a foot Regiment.
Sir John Byron, one Troope of Horſe.[87]

I have omitted the Earle of Cumberland his Horſe and foot, The Marqueſſe Hertfords Horſe and foot The Earle of Darbies Horſe and foot, which is at the leaſt 16000.

None of which have been as yet with His Majeſtie, ſo that in all parts His Majeſties Army of Horſe and Foot is ſuppoſed to be 40000 Souldiers.

[84] Sir Thomas Byron, brother to John, firſt Lord Byron. Dangerouſly wounded at the battle of Hopton Heath, March 19, 1643.
[85] Ludovick Lindſay, fifteenth Earl of Crawfurd in the Peerage of Scotland. Taken priſoner at the battle of Worceſter, Sept. 3, 1651.
[86] George Digby, ſon and heir of John Digby, firſt Earl of Briſtol. Summoned to Parliament in his father's barony of Digby, June 9, 1641. K.G. Died, 1676.
[87] Sir John Byron. Created Lord Byron of Rochdale, co. Lancaſhire, Oct. 24, 1643. Died, 1652.

THE LIST OF THE ARMIE.*

Officers Generall of the Field.

IS Excellency Robert Earle of Eſſex, Captaine Generall.[88]
Philip Skippon Serjeant Major Generall and Preſident of the Councell of Warre.[89]

Captaine James Seigneur Provoſt Marſhall Generall.
Thomas Richardſon Carriage Maſter Generall.

---

* This liſt of the Parliamentary Army exiſts in a ſeparate form as a ſmall 4to. of twenty pages. It varies from the document here reprinted but very ſlightly. As it is very rare, I give the title-page in full.

"The Liſt of the Army Raiſed under the command of his Excellency ROBERT Earle of Eſſex and Ewe, Viſcount Hereford, Lord Ferrers of Chartley Bourchrir and Lovaine: Appointed Captaine General of the Army, Imployed for the defence of the Proteſtant Religion, the ſafety of his Majeſties Perſon and the Parliament, the preſervation of the Lawes, Liberties and Peace of the Kingdom and protection of his Majeſties Subjects from Violence and oppreſſion.

"With the names of the ſeverall Officers belonging to the Army.

"London Printed for John Partredge, 1642."

[88] Robert Devereux, ſon and heir of Robert Devereux, ſecond Earl of Eſſex, who was beheaded for High Treaſon, 1601. Reſtored in blood and honours, July 12, 1603. One of the twenty-ſeven peers who tried Mervin Tuchett, Lord Audley, Earl of Caſtlehaven, 1631. Appointed by the Parliament General of the forces, July 12, 1642. Commanded at the

Officers of the Lord Generalls Train.

Sir Gilbert Gerrard Knight, Treasurer at Warres.
Lionell Copley Esquire, Muster-Master Generall.[90]
Doctour Isaak Dorisla, Advocate of the Army.[91]
Henry Parker Esquire, Secretary of the Army.
Robert Chambers, Auditor of the Army.

---

battle before Worcester, Sept. 23, 1642; Edge Hill, Oct. 23, 1642; the taking of Reading, April 18, 1643; Newbury (first battle), Sept. 19, 1643; Taunton Deane, June 22, 1644. Died, Sept. 14, 1646. Buried in St. John Baptist's Chapel, Westminster Abbey, in a grave where Bohun, Abbot of Westminster, had been buried (temp. Ric. II.), Oct. 19, 1646.—Devereux, *Lives of the Devereux*, ii. 362–470. Oldmixon's *History of the Stuarts*, p. 315.

[89] Philip Skippon is said to have been a man of humble birth; he had served in Holland, where he had raised himself from the rank of a common soldier. He was subsequently one of the Protector Oliver's Council of State. He became possessed of Hirsham, in Sussex, where he was succeeded by his son, Philip Skippon, F.R.S. Arms, gules; five annulets, or.—Clarendon's *Hist.* p. 152. Prestwick's *Respublica*, p. 96.

In the *List of the Army Raised under the command of his Excellency Robert Earle of Essex, &c. London Printed for John Partredge*, 1642, Sir John Merrick is given as filling the place here occupied by Philip Skippon. Clarendon says that Skippon was made Serjeant Major General of the army in the room of Sir John Merrick by the authority of Parliament, "without the chearful concurrence of the Earl of Essex, though Sir John Merrick who had executed that place by his Lordship's choice from the beginning was preferred to be General of the Ordnance."—P. 382.

[90] Lionel Copley, second son of William Copley of Wadworth, co. York. Died in London, Dec. 7, 1675. Buried at Wadworth. More than one member of this family fought on the side of the Parliament. Arms, argent, a cross moline sable. The mottoes borne by the Copleys on their banners were, "For Reformation," and, "Nay, but as a captain of the Host of the Lord am I come."—Hunter's *South Yorkshire*, i. 251.

[91] Isaac Doreslaus, Doreslaer, Dorislaer, or Doorslaer, for the name is spelt thus variously, was son of Abraham Doreslaer; the date and place of his birth are not known. The accompanying table embodies such facts as are recorded of his family:—

Officers Generall of the Horse.

William Earle of Bedford, Lord Generall.[92]
Sir William Belfoore Knight, Lievtenant Generall.[93]

Abraham Doreflaer, a minifter of the Dutch Reformed Church at Oude, Niedorp, in 1602; Eukhuizen in 1605, where he died, March 19, 1655. Author of "A new tranflation of HOLY WRIT with Explanations and notes." Amfterdam, 1614, folio. A "Treatife concerning the differences between the tenets of the Reformed and Anabaptift perfuafions, &c."

1. Samuel Doreflaer, minifter at Wervershoof, 1638; at Brock, in Waterland, 1645; at Delft, 1648, where he died, 1653.

2. Ifaac Doreflaer, minifter at Hensbrock, 1627; at Eukhuizen, 1628, where he died, 1652.

3. David Doreflaer, minifter of the Dutch colonifts in Brazil. Returned to Holland and became minifter at Hobrede and Ofthniazen, 1644; Hultezen, 1649; Tholen, 1650; Zierikzen, 1654. Died, 1671.

Ifaac Doriflaus.

Ifaac Doriflaus was a friend of Sir Henry Mildmay, and the firft Lord Brooke. Through the influence of the latter he was appointed to read a hiftorical lecture in Cambridge; but was foon filenced on account of his maintaining anti-monarchical principles. His great knowledge of Civil Law caufed his nomination to the office of Judge Advocate of the Army. For the fame reafon he was fhortly afterwards made one of the Judges of the Court of Admiralty. He made himfelf efpecially hateful to the Royalifts by affifting to prepare the charge of High Treafon againft Charles I. In the beginning of May, 1649, he failed for Holland as Envoy from the Englifh Parliament to the Hague; he had only fpent a very fhort time there when, on the 12th, or, according to others, the 15th of May, as he was taking his fupper at the Witte Zwaan (White Swan) Inn, fome five or fix men in mafks entered the houfe, blew out the lights in the paffage, and rufhed into the public room, where he, in company with eleven other guefts, was fitting. Two of the confpirators immediately made a murderous attack on a Dutch gentleman named Grijp van Valkenfteyn, fuppofing him to be the Englifh Envoy. Finding out their miftake, however, they fet

[*PARLIAMENT.*]

John Dulbier, Quarter-Mafter Generall.[94]
Sir Edward Dodfworth, Commiffary for the Horfe.
John Ward, Commiffary for the Provifions.
John Baldwine, Provoft Marfhall Generall.[95]

A LIST OF THE TRAIN OF ARTILLERY.

John Earle of Peterborough, Generall of the Ordnance.[96]
Philibert Emanuel de Boyes, Lievtenant Generall of the Ordnance.
Nicholas Cooke, an Affiftant to the Lievtenant of the Ordnance.
Alexander Forboys, a Surveyor or Comptroller.
John Lyon, an Engineer.
Six other Engineers Affiftants.

---

upon Doreflaus, and flew him with many wounds, exclaiming as they did the deed, "Thus dies one of the King's Judges." The leader of this execrable gang was Col. Walter Whitford, fon of Walter Whitford, D.D., of Monkland, in Scotland. He received a penfion for this "generous action" (Wood) after the Reftoration. The Englifh Parliament gave their faithful fervant a magnificent funeral in Weftminfter Abbey, June 14, 1649; but after the Reftoration thofe in power difturbed the body. His duft now refts with that of Admiral Blake, and others fuch as he, in a pit in St. Margaret's Churchyard.—JOHN LODEN GOLLPRIED'S *Kronyck,* iv. 454. VAN DER DA, *Biographifch Woodenbock, in voc.*
There is a portrait of Ifaac Doreflaus by R. Vinkeles.

[92] William Ruffell, fifth Earl of Bedford, fucceeded his father, 1641. Created Duke of Bedford, May 11, 1694. Died, 1700. Commanded the body of referve at Edge Hill, Oct. 23, 1642. Left the Parliamentary fervice and joined the King at Oxford.

[93] Sir William Balfore, Lieutenant of the Tower. Difmiffed from that office, 1640. Commanded the Horfe at Edge Hill, Oct. 23, 1642.

[94] John Dalbier, or Dalbeer, a Dutchman "of name and reputation, and good experience in War," was left out of the newly formed army, and being difcontented, joined the rifing of the Earl of Holland. Killed in an inn at St. Neots, co. Huntingdon, July 5, 1648.

[95] Juftice of peace for Buckinghamfhire, 1650. M.P. for Wendover, 1660.

[96] Henry Mordaunt, fecond Earl of Peterborough, fucceeded to the earldom on the death of his father, June 18, 1642. Died, June 19, 1697. Buried at Turvey, co. Bed.

George Vernon } two Commiffaries of the Ordnance, Materialls,
John Phipps } and Ammunition.

A Commiffary to diftribute Victualls.

Captaine Peter Cannon, a Purveyor Generall, both for Munition and all other neceffaries belonging to the Ordnance.[97]

Eighteen Gentlemen of the Ordnance.

1 Tho. Holyman.
2 Robert Barbar.
3 Patrick Strelley.
4 Adward Wafe.
5 Anthony Heyford.
6 Robert Bower.
7 Henry Edfon.
8 James Francklin.[98]
9 Richard Honey.
10 Jofhua Sing.
11 George Ranfom.
12 Samuel Barry.
13 Daniell Barwick.
14 Tho. Rawfon.
15 Tho. Sippence.
16 Tho. Croffe.[99]
17 Tho. Ayres.
18 William Hickfon.

John Fowke, a Mafter of the Carriages, or Waggon Mafter for the Artillery.

Will. Crawley, a principall Conductor of the Train of Artillery for the Draught-Horfes and Ammunition.

Edward Weft, a Commiffary of the Train of Artillery for the draught-Horfes.[100]

---

[97] An ordinance was forwarded from the Lords to the Commons, 29th Sep., 1645, for "enabling Peter Cannon to make ordnance after a new invention."—*Com. Jour.* iv. 293. According to Walker a perfon named Peter Canon was rector of Rufhton St. Peter's, co. Northampton. "He was an excellent fcholar, a good preacher, and of a good life; and was turned out for reading Common-prayer."—*Sufferings of the Clergy*, 223.

[98] Slain at Exeter.—Sprigg, p. 330.

[99] Slain at the fiege of Sherborne Caftle, Aug. 15, 1645.—*Micro-Chronicon*, 1647.

[100] Edward Weft and William Crawley were "Chiefe conductors of the amunition drought-horfes and traine of artillery" among the Reformados who were felected for the Irifh fervice, June, 1642.—*Broadfide, Brit. Mus.*, 669, f. $\frac{6}{32}$.

[*PARLIAMENT.*]

George Wentworth, a Quarter-Mafter of the Traine of Artillery.
Edward Frodfham ⎫
Henry Roe   ⎬ three Captaines to 600 Pyoners.
John Dungan   ⎭

Gerard Wright   ⎫
Benjamin Hodfon   ⎬ three Lievtenants to 600 Pioneers.
Tho. Williams[101]   ⎭

Lancelet Honiburne, Mafter Gunner.
Chriftopher Troughton, Provoft Marfhall of the Artillery.
Edward Okely, a Battery-Mafter.
Joakim Hane, Fire-worker and Petardier.
William Roberts, Fire-worker and Petardier.
Harman Browning, a Bridge-Mafter for the Traine of Artillery.
Jo. Herdine, an Affiftant unto him.
Lievtenant Generall De Boys, Captaine of 100 Fire-locks.
Rich. Price, Lievtenant to Captaine de Boys.

THE LIST OF THE SEVERALL REGIMENTS OF FOOT AND HORSE.

HIS EXCELLENCIES REGIMENT.

Captaines.

Colonell his Excellency.
Liev. Col. W. Davies.[102]
Sir M. Jo. Bamfield.
Sir Antho. St. John.

Chr. Mathias.
Jo. Skrimpfhiere.
Tho. Skinner.
Roger Bettridge.
Tho. Ward.
Edw. Leventhorp.

---

[101] Slain at Ofweftree, co. Salop, June 15, 1644.

[102] At Newbury, firft battle, "on the parliament's part were flain about 500, colonel Tucker and the Lievtenant colonel of Effex's Regiment."—WHITELOCK, p. 215.

[*ARMY LIST.*]

Lieutenants.	*Enſignes.*
John Rainsford.	John Lloyd.
Fulk Muſket.	Jenkin Song.
Hugh Juſtice.	Edw. Cockram.[103]
Wal. Reed.	Will. Bowen.
Geo. Clark.	Jo. Johnſon.
Alex. Edwards.	Tho. Haſtings.
Jo. Cracroft.	Andr. Ward.
Tho. Lanford.	Hugh Harding.
Hen. Stevens.	

Sir Philip Stapleton[104] Captain of 100 Curaſſiers for his Excellencies Guard.	Captain Nathaniel Draper Captaine to the General's Troop of 50 Carbines.
Adam Baynard Lievtenant.	John Strelley Cornet.
Paul Greſham Quarter-maſter.	Abraham Carter Quarter Maſter.

FIRE LOCKS.

Captains.	*Phyſitian to the Traine and Perſon.*
Robert Turner.	
Ambroſe Tindall.	
Nicholas Devereux.	Doctor John Saint John.[105]

---

[103] Lieutenant Cockeram, ſlain before Scarborough, May, 1645.

[104] Sir Philip Stapleton inherited "but a moderate eſtate in Yorkſhire, and, according to the cuſtom of that country, had ſpent his time in thoſe delights which horſes and dogs adminiſter." A member of the long Parliament; joined in the proſecution of Strafford; oppoſed the ſelf-denying ordinance, 1644. Withdrew beyond ſea, and died at Calais as ſoon as he landed. "Was denied burial upon imagination that he had died of the plague."—CLARENDON, pp. 119, 618.

[105] The perſonal attendant of the Earl of Eſſex.—*Letters of the Devereux,* ii. p. 444.

[*PARLIAMENT.*] 27

Chirurgion to the Traine and Perſon.
Laur. Lowe.

Chirurgion to the Regiment.
William Parkes.

Lieutenants.
Vſeus Martery.
Nich. Halford.
Tho. Lawrence.

Carriage Maſter.
William Wren.

Chaplain.
Stev. Marſhall.[106]

Chaplain for the Regiment of Horſe.
Doctor Burges.[107]

---

[106] Stephen Marſhall, B.D., was born at Godmancheſter and educated at Cambridge, and afterwards held the benefice of Finchfield in Eſſex. He ſpent the laſt two years of his life at Ipſwich. His body was buried in the ſouth aiſle of Weſtminſter Abbey, 23rd Nov. 1655, but was dug up at the Reſtoration.—NEAL's *Hiſt. of the Puritans*, ed. 1822, vol. iv. pp. 133, 319. Pepys ſtates in his Diary, 26th Oct. 1667, that "Mrs. Price tells me that the two Marſhalls at the King's houſe are Stephen Marſhall's, the great Preſbyterian's daughters." The names of theſe two actreſſes, who were ſaid to be women of looſe morals, were Anne and Beche Marſhall. I am not aware that proof has been given that they were in reality the children of this noted preacher.

[107] Cornelius Burgeſs, of the family of Burgeſs of Batcombe, co. Somerſet. Entered the Univerſity of Oxford, 1611. D.D. 1627. One of the moſt popular preachers during the Civil War. Loſt his property at the Reſtoration. Died in extreme want at Watford. Buried in Watford Church, June 9, 1665.

"Wee'l break the windows which the whore
    Of Babylon hath painted,
And when the Popiſh ſaints are doun,
    Then Burgeſs ſhall be ſainted;
There's neither croſſe nor crucifix
    Shall ſtand for men to ſee,
Rome's traſh and trumpery ſhall go down,
    And hey then up go we."
Rump Songs, 1ſt edit. p. 15.

Sir John Merricks Regiment.

Col. Sir Joh. Merrick.[108]
L. C. Vincent Kilmady.
Ser. M. Will Herbert.

Captains.

...... Tyer.
...... Lower.
Fran. Merrick.
Tho. Lawherne.[109]
John Lloyd.

John Edwards.
John Baily.

Provoſt Marſhall.

Iohn Treme.

Chaplain.

...... Tucker.

Chirurgion.

John Woodward.

The Earle of Peterboroughs Regiment.

Col. Jo. E. of Peterborow.
L. C. Sir faithf. Forteſcue.
S. M. Francis Fairfax.

Captains.

Sir Edw. Payton.
Phil. Dutton.
Bevill Prideaux.
Robert Knightley.
Io. Butler.
Hen. Lovell.
Geo. Blunt.

Lievtenants.

Geo. Rowſe.
Rich. Orfice.
Jo. Rice.
Will. Thorp.
Hen. Cafe.
Ornall Fountain.
Tho. Treeſt.
Jo. Balſtone.[110]
Geo. Hartridge.
Jam. Grimes.

---

[108] See note 89.

[109] Thomas Laugherne, or Langhorn, a gentleman of South Wales, had ſerved the Earl of Eſſex as a page in the Low Countries. Deſerted the Parliament in company with Powell and Poyer. He was taken priſoner by Oliver Cromwell in Pembroke Caſtle, July 11, 1648.

[110] This perſon, or a nameſake, was a Lieutenant of foot among the Reformados engaged for the Iriſh ſervice, June, 1642; a Commiſſioner of

[*PARLIAMENT.*] 29

Enſigns.

...... Goldſborow.
John Apew.
Alex. Thory.
Jo. Bridges.

Jam. Harriſon.
Bevill Cruttenden.
Rich. Lidcoat.
Tho. Laham.
Jo. Pew.
Cha. Harrow.

THE EARLE OF STAMFORDS REGIMENT.

Col. Hen. E. of Stamford.[111]
Liev. Col. Edw. Maſſie.[112]
Ser. M. Conſt. Ferrer.

Captains.

Tho. Savill.
Edw. Gray.
Charles Blunt.
Peter Criſpe.
Iſaack Dobſon.
Arnold Coſbie.
Jo. Bird.

Quarter Maſter.

Ferdinando Gray.

Carriage Maſter.

Rich. Phillips.

Lievtenants.

John Clifton.
James Harcus.
William Hewet.
William White.
James Bock.
Robert Hampſon.
Jo. Hemens.
Nath. Tapper.
Robert Mallery.
Hen. Cantrell.

---

aſſeſſment for Norfolk, 1656; and a Captain in the Norfolk Militia in 1659. *Liſt of* .... *Reformados, Brit. Muſ.*, 669, f. $\frac{6}{32}$. *Scobell*, ii. 411. *Com. Jour.* vii. 760.

[111] Henry Grey, ſecond Baron Gray of Groby. Created Earl of Stamford, co. Lincoln, March 26, 1628. Died, Aug. 21, 1673. His ſon, Thomas Grey, commonly called Lord Grey of Groby, died during his father's life, leaving male iſſue.

[112] Edward Maſſey is ſaid to have offered his ſervices to King Charles I. before he was retained by the Parliament. Governor of Glouceſter, which he ſucceſsfully defended againſt the Royal forces. Deprived of his commiſſion by the ſelf-denying ordinance, 1644. Joined King Charles II.; was taken priſoner after the battle of Worceſter, Sept. 3, 1651, but eſcaped abroad.

Chirurgion.
Jo. Rice.

Ensigns.
John Chambers.
John Starkey.
Tho. Griffin.
William Pincock.

James Gray.
Hen. Collingwood.
Tho. Barnes.
James Baker.
Laur. Clifton.

Provost Marshall.
Robert Powell.

The Lord Sayes Regiment.

Col. William Lord Say.[113]
L. C. . . . . Hutchinson.
Ser. M. Ja. Atchafon.

Captains.
Geo. Marrow.
Christo. Burgh.
Jam. Temple.
Walter Lloyd.
Morgan Tinne.
Robert Blowe.
Bussy Basset.

Quarter Master.
Hum. Dix.

Lievtenants.
Iohn Rainsford.
Luke Weekings.

Jam. Hannam.
. . . . . . Hoare.
. . . . . . Langford.
Tho. Haynes.
Wil. Howard.
Jon. Newcomin.
Edw. Cawardine.

Ensigns.
Iohn Butcherfield.
Joseph Farnes.
Io. Kelly.
. . . . . . Corby.
Ben. Lee.
Tho. Colledge.
. . . . . Gittings.
Tho. Sweeper.
Prue. Prideaux.

---

[113] William Fienes, eighth Baron Say and Sele. Created Viscount of Say and of Sele, July 7, 1624. Married Elizabeth, daughter of Thomas Temple of Stow, co. Buckingham, and had issue—1, James; 2, Nathaniel;

The Lord Whartons Regiment.

C. Phil. L. Wharton.[114]
Liev. Col. Jer. Horton.
Ser. Ma. Owen Parry.

Captains.

Robert Long.
Henry Carew.
Jude Leigh.
Henry Skipwith
Chr. Baily.
...... Gibbons.
Elias Struce.

Provoſt Marſhall.

George Higham.

Lievtenants.

Ch. Holcroft.
Fr. Fitſhues.
Edw. Browne.
Tho. Albany.

Wil. Browne.
Will. Bridges.
George Uſher.
William Emerſon.
Anthony Maſham.
Iſaac Turney.

Chirurgion.

Jo. Broughton.

Enſigns.

...... Blake.
Tho. Radford.
Robert Hughes.
Roger Moore.
Wil. Heydon.
Edw. Horton.
Jo. Garret.
Jer. Gardiner.
Rich. Bland.
Edw. Horton.

3, John; 4, Richard; and five daughters, Bridget, Elizabeth, Conſtance, Suſan, and Anne. On the Reſtoration he was made Lord Privy Seal. He died 14th April, 1662.

[114] Philip Wharton, fourth Baron Wharton. Succeeded to the peerage on the death of his grandfather, Philip Wharton, third Baron, 1625. He married, 1, Elizabeth, daughter of Sir Rowland Wandsford, of Pickhay, co. York; 2, Jane, daughter of Arthur Goodwyn of Upper Winchendon, co. Bucks; 3, Anne, daughter of William Carr of .... Scotland. He died 1696.

The Lord Rochfords Regiment.

Col. Lord Rochford.[115]
Liev. C. Ed. Aldrich.
Ser. Ma. Tho. Leighton.

Captains.

Tho. Drake.
George Walsh.
Philip Ballard.
Benjamin Hooke.
Fran. Hudson.
Jasper Brand.
Geo. Willoughby.

Quarter-Master.

Miles Dobson.

Chaplain.

Io. Page.

Lieutenants.

Io. Norship.
William Shawe.
Edw. Deering.

Walter Bradley.
Ralph Carter.
Edw. Melson.
Jo. Sheppard.
Matth. Stoaker.
Humphry Dimock.
Miles Ashton.

Provost Marshall.

Io. Burbeck.

Ensignes.

Henry Newdigate.
Mount Sanders.
Jeffery Lloyd.
Peter Blewin.
Edw. Lovell.
George Burrell.
William Williams.
Hen. Smith.
Jo. Bramston.

Carriage Master.

Io. Poore.

The Lord Saint-Johns Regiment.

Col. Oliver L. St. John.[116]
Liev. Col. Tho. Essex.

Ser. Ma. Ed. Andrews.

---

[115] John Carey, son and heir of Henry Carey, fourth Baron Hunsdon and first Viscount Rochford and Earl of Dover. John Carey succeeded to his father's honours, 1668. Died, 1677. See note 18.

[116] Oliver Saint John, eldest son of Oliver St. John, fourth Baron Saint

[*PARLIAMENT.*]

Captains.
Timo. Neale.
Oliver Beecher.
Jo. Harvie.
Lewis Pemberton.
Tho. Miles.
Jo. Hilderfon.
Tho. Thorogood.

Carriage Mafter.
Tho. Greene.

Quarter Mafter.
William Walwin.

Lievtenants.
Theo. Paholigus.[117]
Will. Boughty.
William Cafie.
Jos. Sears.
Lyon Pilkington.
Tho. Bedealls.
Edw. Carew.

John, who was created Earl of Bolinbroke, co. Lincoln, Dec. 28, 1624; was fummoned to Parliament in his father's barony of Saint John. Slain at Edge Hill, Oct. 23, 1642.

[117] A member of the family of Palæologus of Landulph, co. Cornwall, who are believed to have been a branch of the Imperial houfe of Conftantinople. The Englifh Palæologoi have long been extinct in the male line, both here and in the Weft Indies, to which fome of the members of the family emigrated. Their blood, tranfmitted through females, doubtlefs yet flows in the veins of many a Devonfhire and Cornifh gentleman.

"Fors non mutat genus."

The perfon here indicated may poffibly be Theodore Palæologus, fon of Theodore Palæologus of Landulph, who died Jan. 21, 1636. This Theodore was afterwards a failor, and died at fea in 1693, on board the Royal Charles. From his will, which was proved at Doctors' Commons, it feems that he had no iffue.

The following entry occurs in the Burial Regifter of Weftminfter Abbey. It is probable that it relates to the Theodore Palæologus of Lord St. John's Regiment.

"1644 Theodorus Pahiologus
was b^d near the lady St.
John's tomb May 3."

For information relative to the Englifh Palæologoi, fee the following:—
Archæologia, xviii. pp. 85–104. *Chambers' Journal*, xvii. p. 24. BURN's *Hift. of Foreign Refugees*, p. 230. SCHOMBURGK's *Hift. of Barbadoes*. OLDMIXON's *Weft Indies*. *Gentleman's Magazine*, Jan. 1843. LYSON's *Cornwall*, p. 172. *Notes and Queries*, 1ft Series, *paffim*.

[ARMY LIST.]

Rich. More.
John Wood.
Wendy Oxford.

Provoſt Marſhall.
Robert Lucas.

Chaplain.
Jo. Vinter.

Enſignes.
Io. Marſhall.

Tho. Joy.
Edw. Gravenor.
Geo. Elliot.
Lewis Mordent.
Noah Neale.
Hen. Tayler.
Jos. Scarbrough.
Ric. Parker.
Hen. Lovell.

Chierurgion.
William Roberts.

THE LORD BROOKS REGIMENT.

Col. The Lord Brook.[118]
Liev. Col. Sir Edw. Peto.
S. M. Wal. Ailworth.

Captains.
Tho. Fitch.
Jo. Lilborne.[119]
Ralph Cotsforth.
Tho. Hickman.

Nicho. Warren.
..... Sambridge.
John Bridges.

Waggon-Maſter.
John Smith.

Quarter-Maſter.
John Hunt.

---

[118] Robert Greville, ſecond Baron Brooke. Slain at the ſiege of Lichfield, March 2, 1642.

[119] Son of Richard Lilburn of Thickley-Punchardon, co. Durham. An apprentice to a cloth-packer in Saint Swithin's Lane, London. Became clerk to William Prynne, in or about 1632. Whipped at a cart's tail from the Fleet Priſon to Weſtminſter, and afterwards ſtood in the pillory, for having written a book againſt biſhops. His whole life was one long ſtruggle againſt authority. He died at Eltham, co. Surrey. Buried "in the New Church yard adjoining to Bedlam," Aug. 31, 1657.

John Lilburn's ſtrange doings in the Iſle of Axholme, co. Lincoln, have not hitherto met with the notice they deſerve. See on this matter, *Hiſt. of Thorne,* 1829, 12mo. pp. 150–155. PECK's *Topographical Account of*

[*PARLIAMENT.*]

Lieutenants.	*Enſignes.*
John Aſhfield.	Iohn Davis.
Chriſt. Langton.	Iohn Warren.
Daniel Hinton.	Tho. Roberts.
Nich. Ling.	William Taton.
John Matterſey.	Tho. Hinde.
Jo. Morris.[120]	Hum. Lyeathcock.
Roger Cotterell.[121]	Jo. Peto.
John Gates.	Tho. Ginnings.
. . . . . . Wivell.	. . . . . Cotton.
William Bridges.	. . . . . Eggleſton.
Provoſt Marſhall.	*Chirurgion.*
William Coleman.	Iohn Cleare.

the *Iſle of Axholme*, pp. 117–120. *John Lilburn tried and Caſt*, 4to. 1653, pp. 84–90. Arms, argent, three water-bougets, ſable. Perſons bearing this name, and not improbably of the ſame ſtock, were living in Yorkſhire and Lincolnſhire in the ſixteenth and ſeventeenth centuries. In 1545 Thomas Lelburn was parſon of Atcliffe, co. Lincoln. In 1602 the bell was rung in Louth Church for Edward Lilborne, and Richard Lilburne was a recuſant ſchoolmaſter reſiding at Kirkby Wharf, *circa* 1604. *Louth Ch. Acc.* Peacock's *Rom. Cath. in co. York*, 1604, p. 26.

[120] It is not improbable that this perſon is the John Morris who defended Pontefraɛt Caſtle during its laſt ſiege. It is known that he had ſerved the Parliament, but was left out of the new army after the ſelf-denying ordinance, as "his life of great licence kept not his reputation with the new officers." Pontefraɛt ſurrendered, March 22, 1649. Morris, the governor, was excepted from mercy; he eſcaped, however, for a time, by charging through the enemies' lines on horſeback, but was captured about ten days afterwards in Lancaſhire. Tried at York for high treaſon, Aug. 16, 1649. Executed, Aug. 23. His body reſts in Wentworth Church, co. York, near to the grave of his old maſter the Earl of Strafford.

Arms, azure, three eagles diſplayed, or; on a canton argent, a caſtle, gules.—DUGDALE's *Viſit. of Yorkſhire*, 1665, 1666, p. 267. *Commons' Journals*, vi. p. 174. THORESBY's *Ducatus Leod.* (Whitaker's edit.), p. 71. *Notes and Queries*, iii. s. vol. v. p. 476. DRAKE's *Pontifraɛt Caſtle*, (Surtees' Soc.), p. 86.

[121] Priſoner at Cirenceſter, 2 Feb. 1643.—SOMERS' *Traɛts*, iv. 510.

The Lord Mandeviles Regiment.

Col. Hen. L. Mandevill.[122]
L. Col. Jo. Parkinson.
Ser. Ma. Iohn Drake.

Captaines.

Fran. Wilson.
Hen. Samerster.
Edw. Watts.
Robert Goodwin.
Robert Palmer.
Dan. Redman.
Osborn Williams.

Provost-Marshall.

Iohn Turner.

Carriage-Master.

Robert Ousby.[123]

Lievtenants.

..... Turkington.
John Hoskins.

Roger Whetstone.
Fran. Ballard.
Hen. Worth.
Io. Rose.
Bridges Bushell.
Nich. Dibdale.
Hugh Beeston.
James Blodwell.

Chaplain.

Simon Ash.

Quarter-Master.

Nich. Wood.

Ensignes.

Jasper Goodwin.
Nath. Walmsly.
Tho. Davies.
Io. Ramsey.
Cha. Davies.
Tho. Goodwin.

---

[122] Edward Montague, son and heir of Henry Montague, first Earl of Manchester, was educated at Cambridge. M.P. for Huntingdon in the first Parliament of Charles I. One of the Commissioners to treat with the Scotch, 1640. Defeated the Earl of Newcastle at Horncastle, co. Lincoln, June, 1643. Took Lincoln Castle by storm, Monday, May 6, 1644, capturing therein Sir Francis Fane, the governor, Sir Charles Dallison, and others. Died at Whitehall, May 5, 1671, aged 69 years.

[123] This is an uncommon name, but is found in Westmerland and Cumberland. Robert Ousby, a monk of St. Alban's, was abbot of Burton-on-Trent, and died in 1432.—*Mon. Ang.* iii. 49.

[*PARLIAMENT.*] 37

Math. Milbourn.
..... Fleming.
Iohn Daily.

Chirurgion.

William Stannard.

THE LORD ROBERTS HIS REGIMENT.

Col. John L. Roberts.[124]
L. Col. Will. Hunter.
Ser. M. Alex. Hurry.

Captaines.

James Witcherly.
Io. Walker.
Io. Mercer.
Mark Grimes.
John Mill.
Ionath. Elliot.
Iam. Fookes.

Quarter-Master.

William Rawlins.

Provost Marshall.

Hum. Franouth.

Lievtenants.

Geo. Graden.
Tho. Keckwick.
Rich. Baron.
Walter Heys.
Jo. Melvin.
Tho. Turrell.
Barnard Smelomb.
Io. Spooner.
Dan. Trevor.

Carriage-Master.

Thom. Higgins.

Chaplain.

Dr. Calibut Downing.[125]

---

[124] John Robartes, second Baron Robartes of Truro, co. Cornwall. Succeeded to his father's title, 1634. Created Viscount Bodmin, co. Cornwall, and Earl of Radnor, July 23, 1679. Died at Chelsea, July 17, 1685. Buried at Lanhedrock, co. Cornwall.

[125] The eldest son of Calybute Downing of Shennington, co. Gloucester. Lord of the Manors of Sugarswell and Tysoe, co. Warwick. A commoner of Oriel College, Oxford, 1623. Rector of Hickford, co. Bucks, and of West Ildsey, co. Berks. Exchanged the latter rectory for that of Hackney, near London. Died at Hackney, 1644. Calybute Downing had the misfortune to be the father of George Downing, a man notorious for one of the blackest acts of perfidy to be found in our annals. George Downing began life as a minister of religion, having been Colonel Okey's Chaplain.

Enſignes.

Tho. Rouſe.
William Hender.
Alex. Tulidaffe.
Cuthbert Farley.
Ios. Normington.
Iohn Skudamore.

Mark Grimes.
Edw. Genings.
Ben. Groome.
Iohn Merrick.

Chirurgion.

Edw. Cooke.

COLONELL CHOLMLIES REGIMENT.

Col. Sir Hen. Cholmly.[126]
L. Col. Launce Alured.
Ser. M. Th. Southcot.

Captaines.

Henry Ienkins.
William Bateler.
Henry Katcofe.

Goddard Leigh.
Richard Jones.
Robert Hunt.
Iohn Bury.

Provoſt Marſhall.

Nicholas Garth.[127]

He was afterwards "a ſoldier in Scotland, and at length ſcout Maſter general there, and a burgeſs for ſeverall corporations in that kingdom." He became loyal at the Reſtoration, and was diſpatched as envoy extraordinary into Holland, where, under the promiſe of ſafety, he trepanned Colonel Okey, Miles Corbet, and Colonel Barkſtead into his power, and ſent them over to England to ſuffer death for having been members of the commiſſion for trying King Charles I. George Downing was created a Baronet, July, 1663. Arms, barruly of eight, argent and vert, a griphon rampant, or.

[126] The ſecond ſon of Sir Richard Cholmley of Whitby, co. York. He twice beſieged his brother, Sir Hugh Cholmley, who had deſerted the ſervice of the Parliament, in his caſtle of Scarborough. Survived the Reſtoration, and is ſaid to have been active in bringing about that event.

[127] Nicholas Garth was not improbably a member of the family of Garth of Headlam, co. Durham. The name Nicholas does not occur in the very carefully compiled pedigree by the late John Richard Walbran, Eſq. Arms of Garth of Headlam and of Bolham, co. Durham, or, two lions

[*PARLIAMENT.*]

Lievtenants.
Mich. Jobſon.
Mich. Dane.
William Wellin.
George Fulwood.
Io. Shanke.
Io. Fiſher.
...... Andrewes.
...... Goodwin.
Smith Wilkinſon.

Chaplain.
Adoniram Bifield.

Enſignes.
Hugh Philips.
George Rotherham.
Hen. Burkſley.
Tho. Apleby.
William Weſt.
Barth. Burrell.
Herald Skrimſhaw.

COLONELL HOLLIS HIS REGIMENT.

Col. Denzell Hollis.[128]
L. C. Hen. Billingſley.
Ser. Maj. Jam. Quarls.[129]

Captaines.
Allen Povey.
William Barke.
Richard Lacey.
George Harlock.
Jo. Francis.
Wm. Burles.
...... Bennet.

Lievtenants.
Rich. Parker.
Jo. Court.[130]
Geo. Hampſon.
Roger Noard.
Io. Owen.
Tho. Lawrence.
...... Samuel.
Tho. Churchman.

Enſignes.
Ralph Walſet.

---

paſſant, in pale, between three croſſlets fitchée, ſable.—WALBRAN's *Gainford*, p. 110.

[128] Denzill Holles, younger ſon of John Holles, firſt Earl of Clare. One of the five members charged with high treaſon, 1641. One of the commiſſioners ſent by Parliament to wait on Charles II. at the Hague, 1660.

[129] Killed at Brainford, Nov. 12, 1642.—*Micro-Chronicon.*

[130] A perſon of this name, deſcribed as of Ulnhall, co. Warwick, yeoman, paid 64*l.* 18*s.* on compounding for his eſtate.—*Dring*, 23.

[*ARMY LIST.*]

Rawley Willis.
Edw. Neve.
Tho. Cattorill.

Robert Willoughby.
Tho. Clement.
Alexander Payard.

Colonell Bamfields Regiment.

Col. William Bamfield.[131]
L. C. Sir Ro. Wingfield.
Ser. Ma. Sam. Price.

Captaines.

Rob. Baker.
Rich. Benson.
Io. Iesop.
Io. Minshaw.
Wil. Owen.
Tho. Stafforton.
. . . . . Pawlet.

Chaplain.

. . . . . Freeman.

Chirurgion.

Rich. Searle.

Lievtenants.

Io. Hart.
Ambr. Cade.
Ralph Garth.
Tho. Durdo.
Tho. Latimer.

Hogan Rookwood.
Hum. Burton.
Albion Derickbore.
He. Wray.
Andrew Ball.

Quarter-master.

Chri. Allanson.

Carriage-mast.

He. Beecher.

Ensignes.

Samson Manaton.
George Wingfield.
Sym. Giggins.
Io. Rose.
Io. Browne.
William Blake.
Richard Jackson.
Io. Price.
Fra. Barber.
Tho. Hudson.

Provost Marshall.

Richard Gray.

---

[131] Sir William Bamfield soon joined the King's service, and was taken prisoner at Arundel by Sir William Waller, Jan. 28, 1644. Assisted in the escape of the Duke of York, 1648.

Colonell Granthams Regiment.

Col. Tho. Grantham.[132]
Liev. C. Fran. Clarke.
Ser. Ma. Io. Holman.

Captaines.

Hen. Afhley.
Sir Tho. Pigot.
Rich. Gibbs.
Tho. Rogers.
Fran. Grantham.
Geo. Slatford.
Hen. Blundell.

Quarter-maſt.

H. Throckmorton.

Lieutenants.

Francis Gray.
Edw. Tetlow.
Ifaac Challys.
Thomas Lee.
Steph. Deane.
Edw. Apfeley.

Io. Blanden.
Miles Hitchcock.
Geo. Walter.
Tho. Sparrow.

Provoſt Marſhall.

Robert Gibbons.

Enſignes.

Nethermill Garrard.
Tho. Browne.
Tho. Coo.
Geo. Langford.
Io. Middleton.
Henry Gurney.
Sheldon Napper.
Iob Throckmorton.
Ben. Betfworth.
Tho. Blundell.

Carriage-maſter.

Io. Hopkinfon.

Sir William Constables Regiment.

Col. Sir W. Conftable.[133]
Liev. C. Rob. Grain.
Ser. M. He. Frodfham.

Captaines.

Tho. Eure.

---

[132] Colonel Thomas Grantham reinforced the Parliamentary Army with the troop under his command the evening after Edge Hill battle.

[133] Sir William Conftable of Flamborough, co. York. Knighted by the

[*ARMY LIST.*]

Iam. Breckham.
Io. Fenwick.
Simon Needham.
Ben. Cicill.
Humph. Jones.
Iam. Gray.

Provost Marshall.

Iohn Yarner.

Carriage-Master.

Caleb Love-joy.

Lievtenants.

Edm. Hackluit.
Io. Linch.
..... Sumner.
Io. Dugdaile.
Tho. Compton.
Hen. Pownall.
Tho. Best.
Iacob Stringer.
..... Courtop.

Ro. Harvie.

Chirurgion.

Nath. Harris.

Chaplain.

William Sedgwick.[134]

Ensignes.

Ioseph Smith.
William Knight.
William Miller.
Arthur Young.
..... Lifter.
Arth. Pargiter.
..... Harecourt.
Iohn Gorge.
Tho. Roe.
Moses Neale.

Quarter-master.

William Bradford.

Earl of Essex in Ireland, 1599. Created a Baronet, 1611. Imprisoned in the matter of Shipmoney. He was appointed one of the commissioners for trying Charles I., and signed the death-warrant. He died, 1655. With retrospective malignity, worthy of those who violated the sanctity of the graves at Westminster, his name was excepted out of the general pardon at the Restoration as if he had been living; thus his estates became forfeited. Arms, quarterly, gules and vaire, over all a bend, or.

[134] Son of William Sedgwick of London. Entered Pembroke College, 1624; was chief preacher of the city of Ely during the Commonwealth. He was called, from his zealous labours, "the apostle of the isle of Ely," but gave up his preferment on the passing of the Act of Uniformity.—Wood's *Athenæ Oxon. in voce.*

[*PARLIAMENT.*] 43

Colonell Ballards Regiment.

Col. Tho. Ballard.[135]
Liev. C. Fran. Martin.
Ser. Ma. Wil. Lower.

Captaines.

Tho. Middleton.
Fran. Foukes, fen.
Edward Allen.
Edw. Primrofe.
Pet. Momford.
Io. Browne.
Rob. Noyes.

Quarter-maſt.

Io. Lamſdie.

Lievtenants.

Leon Moreton.
Io. Hughes.
Dan. Redman.
Iohn Lookar.
Fran. Fowke, jun.

Fran. Bowyler.
Edw. Norbury.
Robert Davies.
Tho. Brandy.

Waggon-maſter.

Jere. Burleigh.

Enſignes.

Hen. Collingwogd.
William Fowles.
Cha. Parker.
Robert Purpell.
Henry Higgins.
Tho. Axſtell.
Io. Hardy.
Edw. Wett.
William Ogee.
William Garfoot.

Provoſt-Marſhall.

Ben. Ludlow.

Sir William Fairfax his Regiment.

Col. Sir William Fairfax.[136]
L. Col. Will. Monings.
Ser. Ma. Jarvis Paine.

Captaines.

Francis Rogers.

---

[135] Commander-in-chief in Lincolnſhire for the Parliament, 1643. Afterwards entered the Royal ſervice.
[136] Sir William Fairfax of Steeton, co. York, Knight, eldeſt ſon of Sir

[ARMY LIST.]

Edward Ondingfell.
Thomas Rufh.
Michael Bland.
Robert Wilfhiere.
..... Leighton.
William Trunke.

Quarter-Mafter.

Thomas Tyrer.

Chirurgion.

James Winter.

Lievtenants.

David Goldfmith.
Thomas Whitney.
George Tirwhit.[137]
Iohn Caldecott.
William France.
Thomas Rutton.
Francis Bland.

George Gifford.
William Llewellin.
Iohn Fofter.

Provoft Marfhall.

Henry Fifher.

Enfignes.

Iohn Read.
Atwell Needham.
Iohn Lloyd.
Richard Adams.
Richard Upton.
Edward Otter.
Iames Sleigh.
Io. White.
Theophilus Willey.
Samuel Kenarick.

Carriage-Mafter.

Henry Ward.

Philip Fairfax of Steeton, by his wife Frances, daughter of Edmund Sheffield, third Baron Sheffield of Butterwick, co. Lincoln, and firft Earl of Mulgrave. Sir William Fairfax married Frances, daughter of Sir Thomas Chaloner, Knight, of Guifborough in Cleveland, fifter of Thomas Chaloner and James Chaloner, who were members of the commiffion for trying King Charles I.

Sir William Fairfax was flain before Montgomery Caftle, Oct. 27, 1644. —Thoresby's *Ducatus Leodinenfis*, p. 67. Stonehouse's *Ifle of Axholme*, p. 262.

[137] George Tyrwhitt was a member of the old and illuftrious houfe of Tyrwhitt of Kettilby and Stainfield, co. Lincoln. His name does not occur in the printed pedigree. Many of the members of this family were royalifts; fome others were, in feeling at leaft, on the popular fide. A privately printed hiftory of this family exifts.

[*PARLIAMENT.*] 45

Colonell Charles Essex his Regiment.

Col. Charles Effex.[138]
L. C. Adam Coningham.
Ser. Ma. . . . .

Captaines.

William Roberts.
Jo. Ienkins.
Francis Hall.
William Frederick.[139]
Io. Hafelwood.
Samuel Loftus.
Sir Wil. Effex.

Quarter-maſt.

Rog. Wafe.

Lievtenants.

Francis Hall.
Edward Barnewell.
Iames Webb.
Ralph Williams.
Barth. Elliot.
Walraven Hemert.
Chriftoph. Crow.

Chriftoph. Chidley.
Iames Burrell.
Daniel Robinfon.

Chaplain.

Samuel Wells.

Enſignes.

Io. Shipman.
Leonard Hawkins.
Io. Wheeler.
Io. Warkins.
Tracey Smart.
Io. Withers.
William Stratford.
Thomas Fitz.
Rob. Shergall.
Rich. Thornehill.

Provoſt Mar.

Martin Benthin.

Chirurgion.

Io. Browne.

---

[138] Charles Effex, fon of Sir William Effex of Lambourne, co. Berks (who was himfelf a captain in his fon's regiment). He had been a page to the Earl of Effex, through whofe influence he obtained a command in the Low Countries. Killed by a mufket-fhot at Edge Hill, Oct. 23, 1642, where his father was taken prifoner by the King's forces.

[139] Probably William, eldeft fon of Chriftopher Frederick, Sergeant Surgeon to James I.

Colonell John Hambden his Regiment.

Col. John Hambden.[140]
Liev. C. Wagftaff.
Ser. Ma. Will. Barriff.

Captaines.

Richard Ingoldefbe.[141]
..... Nicholls.
..... Arnett.
John Stiles.
..... Raymant.
Robert Farrington.
..... Morris.

Lievtenants.

Henry Ifham.
A Dutchman.
..... Shorter.

Enfignes.

Edward Willet.
Laurence Almot.

Chaplain.

William Spurftow.[142]

How the number of Souldiers in each Regiment of Foot are divided under their feveral Captaines.

The Colonells company	200
The Lievtenant Colonells company	160
The Sergeant Majors company	140
Seven Captaines	700

Every Regiment confifts of 1200. Befides Officers.

---

[140] John Hampden, eldeft fon of William Hampden of Hampden, co. Bucks, by his wife Elizabeth, fecond daughter of Sir Henry Cromwell of Hinchinbroke, co. Hunt. Wounded at Charlgrove field, June 18, 1643; died fix days afterwards.

[141] Richard Ingoldfby of Lenthenborough, co. Bucks. One of the commiffioners for the trial of Charles I. His fignature is attached to the death-warrant. Pardoned at the Reftoration, and created a Knight of the Bath. His refidence was at Waldridge, in the parifh of Dinton, near Aylefbury. He was buried in Hartwell Church, Sept. 16, 1685.—Noble's *Houfe of Cromwell*, vol. ii. p. 189.

[142] Sometime Mafter of Katherine Hall, Cambridge, but ejefted for refufing "the engagement."—Neal's *Hift. of Puritans*, iv. 375.

[*PARLIAMENT.*]

The Names of the Counsell of Warre.

Sir John Mericke, Prefident.
Sir William Belfore, Lievtenant-Generall of the Horfe.
Colonell Wardlaw.
Colonell Grantham.
Sir William Conftable.
Philibert Emmanuel de Boyfe, Lievtenant Generall of the Artillery.
Doctor Ifaac Dorifla, Advocate of the Army.

HE Lift of the Troops of Horfe, under the command of WILLIAM Earle of BEDFORD : Each Troop confifting of 60 Horfe; befides 2 Trumpeters, 3 Corporalls, a Sadler, and a Farrier.

Colonells and their Officers.

Colonell, William Earle of Bedford.	Colonell, Sir Wil. Belfore.
Major.	Major, Jo. Urrey.
Chirurgion, Hugh Ward.	Chirurg. James Swright.
	Colonell, Bazil Lord Fielding.[143]

---

[143] Bazil Fielding, fon and heir of William Fielding, firft Vifcount Fielding and Earl of Denbigh, fought in the Parliamentary Army at Edge Hill, his father, the Earl of Denbigh, ferving as a volunteer on the fide of the King. William, firft Earl of Denbigh, was mortally wounded in the Royal Army near Birmingham, April 3, 1643, and now lies buried at Monk's Kirby, co. Warwick. Bazil, the fecond Earl, died Nov. 28, 1685.

Major, Robert Beckill.
Colonell, Lord Willoughby of Parham.[144]
Colonell, Sir William Waller.[145]
Major, Horatio Carew.

Chirur. James Bricknell.
Colonell, Edwin Sands.
Major, Alex. Douglas.
Chirurgion, John Anthony.

1 Troop.

The Lord Generalls.
Liev. W. Anfell.
Cornet, John Palmer.

2.

C. Sir W. Belfore.
L. Iohn Meldram.
C. William Jewty.

3.

C. L. Grey, Groub.
L. Sim. Matthews.
C. Th. Barington.
Q. Da. Madox.

4.

C. Earle of Peterb.
L. Herb. Dlaufherd.[146]
C. Will. Cheney.

5.

C. Lord Say.
L. Hen. Atkinfon.
C. John Croker.
Q. Robert Parin.

6.

C. Lord Brooke.
L. Richard Croffe.
C. Rob. Lilbourne.
Q. Io. Okey.

---

[144] Francis Willoughby, fifth Baron Willoughby of Parham. He took Gainfborough by ftorm, July 16, 1643, getting "great ftore of ammunition and armes in the towne, a good part of the Earl of Kingfton's Treafures; one writes, more gold than his red bever hat will hold."—*The Kingdom's Weekly Intelligencer*, 18–25, July, 1643, as quoted in STARK's *Hift. of Gainfborough*, 1843, p. 130. "The Lord Willoughby kept the town afterwards againft the Earl of Newcaftle's forces, till overpowered with numbers he was forced to furrender it on honourable conditions."—WHITELOCK, i. 209. Drowned in the Weft Indies, 1666.

[145] Son of Sir Thomas Waller, Conftable of Dover Caftle. Had ferved in the Low Country wars. He was defeated at the battle of Lanfdowne, July 5, 1643. Died Sept. 9, 1669.

[146] This is almoft certainly a mifprint for Blanfherd.

[*PARLIAMENT.*] 49

7.

C. L. Haſtings.[147]
L. Tho. Gratwick.
C. Hen. Ayfluye.
Q. Tho. Meſham.

8.

C. L. St. John.
L. Marmad. Couper.
C. Oliver Cromwell.
Q. W. Wallen.

9.

C. L. Stanford.
L. Samuel Boſa.
C. Cap. Ric. Bingley.
Q. Tho. Vaves.

10.

C. L. Fielding.
L. Reeve Bayley.
C. Tho. Brudnell.
Q. William Tovey.

11.

C. L. Wharton.
L. Ralph Whiſtler.
C. Peter Ware.
Q. Nich. Batterſby.

12.

C. Lord Willoughby of P.
L. Hum. Brookbank.
C. Tho. Hickman.

13.

C. Lord Grey.
Q. . . . . . Madox.

14.

C. Jam. Sheffeld.[148]
L. Tho. Jewks.
C. Rich. Maunder.
Q. Rich. Iolly.

15.

C. Sir W. Waller.
L. Ric. Newdigate.
C. Foulke Grevill.
Q. Fran. Grey.

16.

C. John Gunter.
L. Hen. Strelly.
C. James Godderd.
Q. Edw. Pudſey.

17.

C. Will. Pretty.

---

[147] Ferdinando Haſtings, ſon and heir of Henry Haſtings, fifth Earl of Huntingdon. Born at Aſhby de la Zouch, Jan. 18, 1608. Died Feb. 15, 1655.

[148] Son of Edmund Sheffield, firſt Earl of Mulgrave, by his ſecond wife, Mariana, daughter of Sir William Irwin, Knight.

H

[ARMY LIST.]

L. Matt. Ploughman.
C. Miles Morgan.
Q. Nich. Smith.

18.

Rob. Burrell.
L. John Greene.
C. Nathaniel Weft.
Q. Thomas Eliot.

19.

C. Francis Dowett.
L. Hen. Saderfon.
C. Tho. Gore.
Q. John Otter.

20.

C. Iames Temple.[149]
L. William Baker.
C. Carax Ling.
Q. Fran. Sharpe.

21.

C. Iohn Bird.
L. Samuel Bofa.

C. Ambr. Rooke.
Q. Jonathan Finch.

22.

C. Mathew Draper.
C. Iohn Strelly.
Q. Abraham Carter.

23.

C. . . . . . Dimock.

24.

C. Horatio Carey.
L. Jonas Vandrufick.
C. George Hutton.

25.

C. Iohn Alured.[150]

26.

C. Iohn Neale.
L. Rob. Brufe.

27.

C. Iohn Hamond.

---

[149] This is probably the James Temple who was one of the commiffioners for the trial of King Charles I. He was tried after the Reftoration, but the extreme penalty of the law was not inflicted. Suppofed to have died in the Tower.

[150] John Alured was a Yorkfhireman, probably a native of Hedon in Holdernefs, which borough he reprefented in the Parliament of 1640. He was one of King Charles I.'s judges, and figned the warrant for his execution. Although he died before 1660, his name was put in the act of attainder that his property might be forfeited. His brothers, Lancelot and Matthew Alured, were active on the fide of the Parliament.

[*PARLIAMENT.*] 51

C. William Gill.
Q. Isack Cavaler.

28.

C. Ed. Ayscough.
L. Thomas Mosley.
C. .... Sayer.
Q. .... Clarke.

29.

C. Alex. Pym.
L. Arnold Haward.
C. Ric. Compton.
Q. Ralph Romitree.

30.

C. Iohn Hotham.[151]

31.

C. Arthur Evelin.
L. C. John de la Hay.

32.

C. Geo. Thompson.
L. John Coshe.
C. Iohn Upton.
Q. Will. Couse.

---

[151] Sir John Hotham, Knight, was created a baronet, January 14, 1621. He was Governor of Hull at the breaking out of the Civil War, and refused King Charles I. admittance into that town, March 23, 1642, for which he was proclaimed a traitor by the King. He and his son, Sir John Hotham, Knight, were afterwards discovered to be corresponding with the Earl of Newcastle and other Royalists, for which acts they were tried and suffered death, 1645. Sir John Hotham represented a good old Yorkshire family. He had five wives—1, Katherine, daughter of Sir John Rhodes of Barlborough, co. Derby; 2, Anne, daughter of Ralf Rookesby [Rokeby], a far-away kinswoman of the Editor's; 3, Frances, daughter of John Legard of Ganton, co. York; 4, Katherine, daughter of Sir William Bamborough of Ousan, co. York; 5, Sarah, daughter of Thomas Anlaby of Etton, co. York. John Hotham the younger was son of his first wife: he was married thrice—1, to Frances, daughter of Sir John Wray of Glentworth, Baronet; 2, to Margaret, daughter of Thomas, Viscount Emeley; 3, to Isabell, daughter of Sir Henry Anderson of Long Cowton, co. York. The arms of Hotham are Barry of ten argent and azure, on a canton or, a Cornish chough sable, legged gules.—*Visit. Ebor.* 336.

The register of All Hallows, Barking, contains the following entries:—
"1644-5, Jan. 1, John Hotham, Esqir. Beheaded for betraing his trust to ye state."
"Jan. 2, Sr. John Hotham, Knight, Beheaded ffor betraing his trust to the parlt."

33.

C. Edwin Sandys.
L. John Cockaine.

34.

C. Anth. Milemay.
L. Hen. Hatcher.
C. Sam. Cofworth.
Q. Th. Varnon.

35.

C. Ed. Kyghley.
L. W. Cooker.
C. Tho. Loftus.
Q. Alex. Winchefter.

36.

C. Nath. Fines.[152]

37.

C. Edw. Berry.
L. C. Ed. Saunders.
C. Tho. Billiard.
Q. Hen. Woodnoth.

38.

C. Alex. Douglas.

39.

C. Tho. Lidcott.
L. Rob. Stradling.

---

[152] Nathaniel Fienes, fecond fon of William, eighth Baron, and firft Vifcount Say and Sele, by his wife Elizabeth, daughter of John Temple of Stow, co. Bucks. He was one of the committee nominated by Parliament to accompany Charles I. into Scotland. Defeated by Prince Rupert near Worcefter, Sept. 23, 1642. Governor of Briftol, which he furrendered to Prince Rupert, July 26, 1643, for which act of reputed cowardice he was tried and condemned to death, but pardoned. Keeper of the Great Seal to the Protector Richard Cromwell. He married Elizabeth, daughter of Sir John Elliot of Port Elliot in Cornwall. Died at Newton Toney, near Salifbury, Dec. 16, 1669.

The cavaliers made merry over the defeat of Fienes and his followers before Worcefter. More than one piece of doggerel relating to this adventure has come down to modern times:—

> "Thither came Fines, with armes complete,
> The town to take and Byron defeat,
> Provifions were made but he ftaid not to eat,
>   Which no body can deny.
>
> "But as foon as he heard our great guns play,
> With a flea in his ear he run quite away,
> Like the lawfull begotten fon of Lord Say,
>   Which no body can deny."

[*PARLIAMENT.*]   53

40.

C. Tho. Hamond.
L. John Lindfey.
C. Mi. Wanderford.

41.

C. John Dulbeir.[153]
L. Wil. Framton.
C. H. Vanbraham.
Q. Io. Downeham.

42.

C. Francis Fines.
L. Iames Moore.
C. Henry Fines.
Q. George Malten.

43.

C. S. A. Hafelwrick.[154]
L. Jervis Brakey.

C. Tho. Horton.
Q. Zach. Walker.

44.

C. S. Walt. Earle.
L. Ed. Iohnfon.
Q. Paul Scooler.

45.

C. Jo. Fleming.
L. Robert Kirle.
C. Ed. Fleming.
Q. B. Blackborow.

46.

C. Ar. Goodwin.
L. Iohn Browne.
C. Peter Palmer.
Q. William Jucey.

---

[153] Moft probably the Col. Dalbier who affifted in the taking of Bafing Houfe, Oct. 1645. He was a Dutchman by birth, and it was from him that Oliver Cromwell "learned the mechanical part of foldiering." In July, 1648, he had deferted to the Royalifts, and was killed in a fkirmifh at St. Neots.—CARLYLE's *Cromwell*, i. 192, 198, 276.

[154] Sir Arthur Hafilrigge, Bart., eldeft fon of Sir Thomas Hafilrigge of Nofeley, co. Leicefterfhire. Brought forward the bill in the Houfe of Commons for the attainder of the Earl of Strafford. One of the five members accufed by King Charles I. of high treafon. The foldiers of Sir Arthur's troop were "fo prodigioufly armed, that they were called by the other fide the regiment of lobfters, becaufe of their bright iron fhells."— CLARENDON's *Hift.* p. 402. They were, neverthelefs, defeated by the Royal army at Roundway Down, July 5, 1643, where Sir Arthur was badly wounded. He was one of King Charles I.'s judges, but did not fign the death-warrant. He died in the Tower fhortly after the Reftoration.

47.

C. Rich. Grenvile.
L. Cha. Fountaine.
C. Jo. James.
Q. Alex. Davifon.

48.

C. Tho. Terrill.
L. William Spry.
C. Iofeph Ianes.
Q. Ed. Throwley.

49.

C. Iohn Hale.
L. Chenie Fuller.[155]
C. I. Midehoope.
Q. Michael Hale.

50.

C. H. Milmay of G.[156]
L. Hen. Gibb.
C. Rob. Milmay.
Q. Edm. Hadon.

51.

C. Will. Balfoore.
C. George Weft.

52.

C. George Auftin.

53.

C. Adrian Scroope.[157]
L. William Day.
C. Max Vetty.
Q. Henry Nuby.

54.

C. Herc. Langrifh.
L. Io. Dingley.

---

[155] Prifoner at Cirencefter 2 Feb. 1643.—SOMERS' *Tracts*, iv. 515.

[156] Henry Mildmay of Graces, co. Effex, a relative of Sir Henry Mildmay, Knight, of Mutfho, co. Effex, who was one of Charles I.'s judges, but did not fign the warrant for execution.

[157] A member of one of the moft important of the knightly families of England. The Scropes were long fettled at Bolton, co. York; other branches of the houfe have dwelt at Mafham, co. York; Cockrington, co. Lincoln; Caftle-Combe, co. Wilts; and Wormfley, co. Oxford, of which laft Adrian Scrope was a member. He ferved the Parliament faithfully throughout the war, and afterwards fat as one of the commiffioners for trying the King, whofe death-warrant he figned. For this he fuffered death after the Reftoration. Arms, azure, a bend, or.

The prefent reprefentative of the houfe of Scrope is Simon Thomas Scrope, Efq., of Danby, co. York, and of Cockrington, co. Lincoln.— SHIRLEY'S *Noble and Gentlemen of England*, p. 287. NOBLE'S *Regicides*, vol. ii. p. 200. BLORE'S *Rutlandfhire*, fol. 1811, pp. 5–8.

[*PARLIAMENT.*]

C. J. de la Blancheur.
Q. Io. Ealfinan.

55.

C. Edw. Wingate.[158]
L. Tho. Evans.
C. Hen. Daldorne.
Q. Io. Whitebread.

56.

C. Edw. Baynton.

57.

C. Ch. Chichefter.
L. Jo. Hyde.
C. Edward Weeks.
Q. Richard Gourd.

58.

C. Hen. Ireton.[159]
L. Jo. de Gennis.
C. Samuel Clarke.
Q. Chrift. Brifton.

59.

C. Walt. Long.
L. Nic. Batterfby.
C. Coniers Cooper.
Q. Walt. Harcourt.

60.

C. John Fines.
L. Jo. Carmichaell.
C. Edw. Walley.
Q. Wil. Bugflock.

61.

C. Fr. Thompfon.
L. Tho. Elliot.
C. Vincent Corbet.
Q. Phil. Barley.

62.

C. Edmond Weft.

63.

C. Sir Robert Pie.

---

[158] Prifoner at Cirencefter 2 Feb. 1643.—SOMERS' *Tracts*, iv. 515.

[159] Henry Ireton, eldeft fon of German Ireton of Attenton, co. Notts. Born, 1610. Gentleman commoner of Trinity College, Oxford, 1626. B.A. 1629. Married Bridget, eldeft daughter of Oliver Cromwell, 1646. Taken prifoner at the battle of Nafeby, but made his efcape during the confufion of the Royalifts' retreat. Made prefident of Munfter, Jan. 1650. Died of the plague before Limerick, Nov. 26, 1651. His body was brought to England and lay in ftate at Somerfet Houfe. Buried in Henry VII.'s Chapel, Weftminfter Abbey, Feb. 6, 1652. After the Reftoration it was taken up and expofed upon a gallows at Tyburn. The trunk was there buried, the head fet up on Weftminfter Hall.—NOBLE'S *Cromwell*, vol. ii. pp. 319-323.

[ARMY LIST.]

64.

C. Thomas Hatcher.

65.

C. Robert Vivers.

66.

C. William Anfelme.

67.

C. Oli. Cromwell.[160]
L. Cutb. Baildon.
C. Jos. Waterhoufe.
Q. Io. Difbrow.

68.

C. Robert Kirle.
L. Ch. Fleming.
C. Iames Kirle.
Q. Iohn Ball.

69.

C. Sir William Wray.

70.

C. Wil. Pretty.

L. Mat. Plowman.
C. Miles Morgan.
Q. Ant. Arundel.

71.

C. Sir Io. Sanders.
L. Wil. Wardley.
C. Math. Pedar.
Q. John Harding.

72.

C. Thomas Temple.

73.

C. Valen. Watton.[161]
L. Jarvis Bonner.
C. . . . . . Watton.
Q. Obadiah Crifp.

74.

C. Sir Faithful Fortefcue.

75.

C. Simon Rudgley.
L. Lew. Chadwick.
C. Edward Fines.

---

[160] Afterwards His Highnefs the Lord Protector. Oliver Cromwell, whofe name occurs as a cornet in Lord St. John's troop, No. 8, is the eldeft fon of Oliver Cromwell, Efq., M.P. for Cambridge, fo foon to be famous. Oliver Cromwell, junior, was baptized Feb. 1623. He died, or was killed during the war.—CARLYLE's *Cromwell*, i. p. 92.

[161] Valentine Wauton, or Walton, of Great Stoughton, co. Hunt. Married Margaret, the fifter of Oliver Cromwell the Protector; was a member of the Court of High Commiffion for trying the King, and figned the warrant. Died in Flanders, 1661.

[*PARLIAMENT.*]

Dragooneers, Each Troope consisting of 100 Horse, Besides the Officers.

1.

Colonell, and Cap. Jo. Browne.
Major & Cap. Nath. Gordon.
Sir John Browne, Captaine.

2.

Cap. Rob. Mewer.
Lievt. Thomas Mewer.
Cor. Nicholas Mewer.

3.

Cap. William Buchain.
Cap. Robert Marine.
Lievt. Francis Bradbury.

Quarter-mafter, Iohn Blackman.
Provoft-Marfhall, Daniel Lyon.

4.

Cap. Sir Anthony Irby.
Lievt. William Patrick.
Cor. Richard le Hunt.

5.

Colonell, James Wandlo.
Lievt. George Dunlas.
Cap. Alexander Nerne.
Cap. Iohn Barne.
Cap. Iames Stenchion.
Chirurgion, Iames Heithley.

Thofe Officers that are not mentioned in thefe Lifts, have not as yet received their Commiffions by reafon of their fuddain imployment in the Expedition.

A true Copie of the Inſtructions agreed upon by the Lords and Commons aſſembled in Parliament, and ſent to his Excellency the Earle of Eſſex Lord Generall of the Army, concerning the advancing of his Forces towards His Majeſty, &c.

IRST you ſhall carefully reſtraine all Impieties, Prophaneneſſe, and Diſorders, Ryot, Inſolence, and Plundering in your Souldiers, as well by ſtrict and ſevere puniſhment of ſuch offences, as by all other meanes which you in your wiſedomes ſhall thinke fit.

Secondly, your Lordſhip is to march with ſuch forces as you thinke fit towards the Army, raiſed in his Majeſties Name againſt the Parliament and Kingdome, and with them, or any part of them, to fight at ſuch time and place as you ſhall judge to conduce to the peace and ſafety of the Kingdom ; And you ſhall uſe your utmoſt endeavours by Battaile or otherwiſe to reſcue his Majeſties perſon, and the perſons of the Prince, and Duke of Yorke, out of the hands of thoſe deſperate perſons who are now about them.

Thirdly, you ſhall take an opportunitie in ſome ſafe and honourable way, to cauſe the Petition of both Houſes of Parliament herewith ſent unto you, to be preſented unto his Majeſtie, and if his Majeſtie ſhall pleaſe thereupon to withdraw himſelfe from the forces now about him, and to reſort to the Parliament, you ſhall cauſe all theſe forces to diſband, and ſhall ſecure and defend his Majeſtie with a ſufficient ſtrength in his returne.

Fourthly, you ſhall publiſh and declare, that if any, who have been ſeduced by the falſe aſperſions caſt upon the proceedings of the Parliament, as to aſſiſt the King in the acting of thoſe dangerous Counſels, ſhall willingly within ten dayes after ſuch publication in the Army, returne to their dutie, not doing any hoſtile act within the time limited, and joyne themſelves with the Parliament, in defence of Religion, his Majeſties perſon, the Liberties and Lawes of the Kingdome, and priviledges of Parliament, with their perſons and Eſtates, as the Members of both Houſes, and the reſt of the Kingdome have done : That the Lords and Commons will be ready upon their ſubmiſſion to receive ſuch perſons in ſuch manner as they ſhall have cauſe to acknowledge they have been uſed with clemency and favour : Provided, that this ſhall not extend to admit any man into either Houſe of Parliament who ſtands ſuſpended, without giving ſatisfaction to the Houſe whereof he ſhall be a Member : and except all perſons who ſtand impeached, or particularly Voted in either Houſe of Parliament for any delinquency whatſoever ; Excepting likewiſe ſuch Adherents of thoſe who ſtand impeached in Parliament of Treaſon, as have been eminent perſons and chiefe Actors in thoſe Treaſons ; And except the Earle of Briſtoll, the Earle of Cumberland, the Earle of New-Caſtle, the Earle Rivers, Secretary Nicholas, Maſter Endimion Porter, Maſter Edward Hide, the Duke of Richmond, the Earle of Carnarvan, the Lord Viſcount Newarke, the Lord Viſcount Faulkland, being one of the principall Secretaries of State to his Majeſtie.

Fifthly, you ſhall apprehend the perſons of all theſe who ſtand impeached in Parliament, or have been declared Traytors by both or either Houſe of Parliament, or other Delinquents, and you ſhall ſend them unto the Parliament to receive condigne puniſhment according to their offences.

Sixthly, you ſhall receive the Loanes, or Contributions of Money, Plate, or Horſe from all his Majeſties loving Subjects, which they ſhall be willing to make for the ſupport of the charge of the Army, and better diſcharge of the ſervice of the Common-wealth ; And you ſhall certifie all ſuch ſummes of Money, and the value of ſuch Horſes, that the perſons thereupon may have the publique faith for payment to be made unto them, as to others of his Majeſties Subjects upon the ſubſcription of Money, Plate, and Horſe.

Seventhly, you ſhall carefully protect all his Majeſties loving

Subjects from rapine and violence by any of the Cavaliers, or other of his Majesties pretended Army, or by any of the Souldiers of the Army which you command; and you shall cause the Armour and Goods of any person to be restored to them from whom they have been unjustly taken.

Eighthly, you shall observe such further Directions and Instructions as you from time to time receive from both Houses of Parliament.

A List of his Majesties Navie Royall, and Merchants Ships; Their Names, Captaines, and Lievtenants, their Men and Burthens in every one, now setting forth for the Guard of the narrow Seas, and for Ireland this yeare 1642.

THE KINGS MAJESTIES SHIPS: THE NAMES OF CAPTAINES, AND LIEVTENANTS, SHIPS, MEN, AND BURTHENS.

1.

IN the JAMES, Robert Earle of Warwicke, Vice-Admirall, Master Slingsby Lievtenant, 260 men, burthen 875 tun.

2. In the SAINT GEORGE, William Batten Captaine, Master William Smith Leivtenant, 260 men, burthen, 792 tun.

3. In the RAINE-BOW, Sir John Menns Captaine, Master Lutten Lievtenant, 260 men, burthen 721 tun.

4. In the Reformation, Sir David Murrey Captaine, Master Standsbuy Lievtenant, 260 men, burthen 731 tun.

[*NAVY LIST.*]

5. Victory, Captaine Fogge Captaine, Master Fogge Lievtenant, 240 men, burthen 742 tun.

6. Henrietta Maria, Captaine Hatch Captaine, Master Wattes Lievtenant, 250 men, burthen 793 tun.

7. Unicorn, Captaine Frenchfield Captaine, Master Sommerston Lievtenant, 250 men, burthen 767 tun.

8. ...... Charles Swanley Captaine, Master Darey Lievtenant, 250 men, burthen 810 tun.

9. Vantguard, Captaine Blith Captaine, Master Blith Lievtenant, 250 men, burthen 751 tun.

10. Entrance, Captaine Owen Captaine, Master Bowen Lievtenant, 160 men, burthen 539 tun.

11. Garland, Captaine Stingsby Captaine, Master Walters Lievtenant, 170 men, burthen 767 tun.

12. Lyon, Captaine Prisse Captaine, Master Hill Lievtenant, 170 men, 602 tun.

13. Antelope, Captaine Burley[162] Captaine, Master Willeby Lievtenant, 160 men, burthen 512 tun.

14. Mary Rose, Captaine Fox Captaine, 100 men, burthen 321 tun.

15. Expedition, Captaine Wake Captaine, 100 men, burthen 301 tun.

16. Greyhound, Captaine Wheler Captaine, 50 men, burthen 126 tun.

---

[162] A member of a good family in the Isle of Wight, where he retired when put out of his command on the navy declaring against the King. During the King's imprisonment in that island he chanced to be at Newport, where he heard an account, probably much exaggerated, of the indignities which the King had to suffer, "and was so much transported with ..... fury, being a man of more courage than of prudence or circumspection, that he caused a drum to be presently beaten, and put himself at the head of the people who flocked together, and cried, 'For God, the king, and the people!' and said 'he would lead them to the Castle and rescue the king from his captivity.'" Captain Burley was, for this rash act, tried for high treason, and suffered the extreme penalty of the law.— CLARENDON's *Hist.* p. 629.

Merchant Ships.

1. In the Martane, Captaine George Martaine Captaine, Master Hakriger Lievtenant, 210 men, burthen 700 tun.
2. Samson, Captaine Ashly Captaine, Master Andrew Lievtenant, 180 men, burthen 600 tun.
3. Cæsar, Captaine Elias Jorden Captaine, Master Norton Lievtenant, 180 men, burthen 600 tun.
4. London, Captaine John Stephens Captaine, Master Pomroy Lievtenant, 180 men, burthen 600 tun.
5. Unicorne, Captaine Edward Johnson Captaine, 143 men, burthen 475 tun.
6. Mary Flower, Captaine Peter Andrews Captaine, 121 men, burthen 450 tun.
7. Bonny Venter, Captaine George Swanly Captaine, 120 men, burthen 400 tun.
8. The Prosperous, Captaine William Driver Captaine, 120 men, burthen 400 tun.
9. Hurclens, Captaine Mover Captaine, 150 men, burthen 350 tun.
10. Paragon, Captaine Leonard Harris Captaine, 105 men, burthen 350 tun.
11. Hopefull Luke, Captaine Lee Captaine, 105 men, burthen 350 tun.
12. Golden Angell, Captaine Walker Captaine, 105 men, burthen 350 tun.
13. Exchange, Captaine Lucas Captaine, 89 men, burthen 325 tun.
14. Mayden-head, Captaine Lewton Captaine, 90 men, burthen 300 tun.
15. Providence, Captaine William Swandly Captaine, 81 men, burthen 271 tun.
16. Jocelyn, Captaine Partridge Captaine, 60 men, burthen 200 tun.

His Majesties Ships for the Irish Seas.

1. The Swallow, Captaine Thomas Kettley, 150 men, 160 tun.
2. Bonny Venture, Captaine Henry Stradling, 160 men, 557 tun.

Merchant Ships.

1. Difcovery, Captaine John Brok-haven, 144 men, 380 tun.
2. Ruth, Captaine Robert Conftable, 120 men, 400 tun.
3. Employment, Captaine Thomas Afly, 132 men, 440 tun.
4. Peter, Captaine Peter Stroung, 81 men, 270 tun.
5. Pennington, Captaine Jofeph Jordan, 300 men, 135 ton.
6. Fellowfhip, Captaine Thomas Colle, 87 men, 290 tun.
7. Mary, Captaine William Capell, 30 men, 163 tun.
8. John, Captaine John Thomas, 15 men, 50 tun.

The Names of the Orthodox Divines, prefented by the Knights and Burgeffes of feverall Counties, Cities, and Burroughs, as fit perfons to be confulted with by the Parliament, touching the Reformation of Church-Government and Liturgie, Aprill 25, 1642.

JAMES Archbifhop of Armagh. Doctor Stiles, Parfon of St. Georges neere the Bridge, prefented by the Burgeffes for the Univerfitie of Oxford.

Doctor Brownrigge, Mafter of Katherine Hall. Doctor Ward, Mafter of Sidney Colledge, prefented by the Burgeffes for the Univerfitie of Cambridge.

Doctor Twift. William Reyner, prefented for Berkfhire.

[NAMES OF ORTHODOX DIVINES.]

Henry Wilkinson. Thomas Valentine, prefented for Buckinghamfhire.

Thomas Dillingham. Oliver Boles, prefented for Bedfordfhire.

Doctor Thomas Wincope. Mafter Thomas Goodwyn, prefented for Cambridgefhire.

Doctor Hoyle. Mafter Bridges of Yarmouth, prefented for Cumberland.

Mafter Gamon. Mafter John Hicks of Lawrick, prefented for Cornwall.

Doctor Innefton. Mafter William Morton,[163] prefented for Durham.

Mafter Levir of Rippon. Mafter Michlethwaite of Cherry Burton, prefented for Eboracens.

Stephen Marfhall of Finchfield. Obediah Sedgewick of Cogfhall, prefented for Effex.

Mafter William Mewe of Eftington, B.D. Mafter John Duninge of Coldafton, prefented for Gloucefterfhire.

Mafter John Greene of Pencombe. Mafter Stanley Gower of Bracton, prefented for Hereford.

Doctor Smith of Barkway. Doctor Burgeffe of Waterford, prefented for Hertfordfhire.

Mafter Thomas Bathurft. Mafter Philip Nye, prefented for Huntington.

Mafter Francis Tailor. Mafter Wilfon of Otham, prefented for Kent.

Mafter Edward Calamy of the Parifh of Aldermanbury. Mafter George Walker of St. John's Parifh. Mafter Caroll of Lincolnes Inne. Mafter Lazarus Seaman of Alhallowes Bredftreete, prefented for London.

---

[163] "In the beginning of the war, Mr. Morton, a very worthy man, left Newcaftle, went into the Parliament's army, and was one of the divines in the Affembly at Weftminfter." He was in attendance on Sir Arthur Hafelrig's troop when it entered Worcefter in 1642.—*Mem. of Ambrofe Barnes (Surtees' Soc.)*, p. 128.

[*NAMES OF ORTHODOX DIVINES.*] 65

Anthony Tuckney of Bofton.[164] Thomas Coleman[165] of Blyton, prefented for Lincolne.

Doctor Harris Warden of Winchefter Colledge. Mafter Morley, prefented for Munmouth.

Doctor Downing of Hackney. Mafter Jeremiah Burroughes, prefented for Middlefex.

Mafter Reignolds Parfon of Branfton. Mafter Hill Parfon of Titchmarfh, prefented for Northampton.

Mafter John Jackfon of Grayes Inne. Mafter William Carter of London, prefented for Northumberland.

Mafter Thomas Thoroughgood. Mafter John Arrowfmith, prefented for Norfolk.

Doctor Sanderfon of Boothby. Mafter John Foxcroft of Gotham, prefented for Nottingham.

Mafter Robert Harris, B.D. Parfon of Hanwell. Mafter Robert Croffe, B.D. fellow of Lincolne Colledge, prefented for Oxford.

Mafter Samuel Gibfon. Mafter Jeremie Whittaker, prefented for Rutland.

Mafter Samuel Crook of Wranton, B.D. Mafter John Connant of Livington, B.D. prefented for Somerfet.

Mafter Thomas Young of Stowmarket. Mafter John Phillips of Wrentham, prefented for Suffolke.

John Langley, Rector of Weftudeley. Chriftopher Tifdale, Rector of Uphufborne, prefented for Southampton.

Doctor Staunton of Kingefton. Doctor Featly of Lambeth, prefented for Surrey.

---

[164] Anthony Tuckney, D.D. was born at Kirton in Holland in 1599. He is faid to have been a relative of John Cotton, who was vicar of Bofton, 1612–1633.—THOMPSON, *Hift. Bofton*, 171.

[165] Thomas Coleman was born in Oxford, and educated at Magdalen Hall in that Univerfity. He was fo accomplifhed a Hebrew fcholar that he went by the name of Rabbi Coleman. He left Blyton in 1642, being, as it is ftated, perfecuted by the Cavaliers. He was afterwards rector of St. James's, Cornhill, London. His death took place in 1647.—WOOD, *Ath. Oxon. fub nom.*

Mafter Edward Corbet of Oxford, M. of Arts. Mafter Samuel Hilderfham, prefented for Salop.

Francis Cook of Yoxhall, Clerk. John Lightfoot of Afhley, Clerk, prefented for Stafford.

Mafter Benjamin Pickering. Mafter Henry Nye, prefented for Suffex.

Mafter Arth. Salway. Doctor Prideaux, Bifhop of Worcefter, prefented for Wigorn.

Mafter Henry Hall, B.D. Mafter Henry Hutton, Mafter of Arts, prefented for Weftmerland.

Henry Seuder, Rector of Collingborne, B.D. Thomas Baily, Rector of Manningford, B.D. prefented for Wiltfhire.

Mafter Burgeffe, Parfon of Sutton Ulfield. Mafter Richard Vines, Parfon of Weddington, prefented for Warwick.

Mafter Richard Buckley, B.D. for Anglefey.

Doctor Temple of Batterfey, for Brecknoc.

Mafter Shute of Lumberftreet, for Cardigan.

Mafter Nicholfon, for Carmarthen.

Mafter Cattarne, for Carnarvan.

Ric. Lloide D.D. for Denbigh.

Doctor Chriftopher Pafhley, for Flint.

Henry Tozer, B.D. and fenior Fellow of Ex. Colledge, for Glamorgan.

Mafter William Spurftoe, for Merioneth.

Mafter Francis Channel, for Pembroke.

Meedw. Ellis, Rector of Guilsfeild, for Montgome.

Doct. Hatchet, for Radnor.

Ifles of Garnfey and Jerfey, Samuel de la Place. Jo. de la March.

The Commiffioners of the generall Affembly have chofe 3 Elders and 6 Minifters to be at this Affembly. The Minifters are Mr. Hinderfon, Mr. Duglaffe, Mr. Rutherfurd, Mr. Bayly, Mr. Gelafpe, and Mr. Borthvicke, who is at London. The Elders are the Earl of Caffels, L. Maitland, and Sr Archib. Johnftone.

[LIST OF FIELD-OFFICERS.]

A LIST of the Field-Officers chosen and appointed for the Irish Expedition, by the Committee at Guild-Hall London, for the Regiments of 5000 foot and 500 horse; Under the Command of PHILIP Lord Wharton, Baron of Scarborough, Lord Generall of Ireland.

TROOPS OF HORSE.

Colonell Generalls Troop.

Captaine, Ralfe Whistler.
Cornet, Peter Ware.
Quarter-master, Nicholas Batterfby.
Corporals { Conyers Cooper.
  Bartho. Johnson.
  Ralph Henery.

Second Troope, Lord Broghill.
Lievtenant, John Allen.
Cornet, Cecill Ashcough.
Quarter-master, Tho. Hudson.
Corporalls { Geo. Staples.
  Robert Bennet.
  Thomas Allen.

Third troop, Sir Faithfull Fortescue.
Lievtenant, Francis Dovet.
Cornet, Tho. Fortescue.

Quarter-master, Jo. Coyshe.
Corporals { Jo. Vangerich.
  Jo. Marshall.
  Ralph Walcot.

Fourth troop, Liev. Colonel Jo. Hurry.
Lievtenant, William Mercer.
Cornet . . . . . Sedefcue.
Quarter-master, Jo. Pearne.
Corporals { Ralph Vickerman.
  Rich. Whymper.
  Will. Crane.

Fifth troop, Alexander Nayrne.
Lievtenant, William Hyde.
Cornet, Marmaduke Cooper.
Quarter-master, Gideon Lock.
Corporals { Nath. Walmsley.
  Hugh Farr.
  Ben. Ballard his Ensigne.

Sixth troop, Jo. Trenchard.
Lievtenant, Adam Baynard.
Cornet, Jo. Hyde.
Quarter-mafter, Francis Fook.
Corporals { Jo. Freake.
           { Jo. Starkey.
           { Tho. Gwalter.

Seventh troop, William St. Leger.
Lievtenant, Ed. Leventhorp.
Cornet, ... Skrynfheere.
Quarter-mafter, Philip Vanderhiden.
Corporals { Ed. Gray.
           { Nicho. Phipp.
           { Robert Wood.

FOOT COMPANIES.

Colonell Generall.
His Captain, Edward Maffey.
His Enfigne, Oliver Cromwell.[166]
Lievtenant Colonell and Sergeant Major Generall, Jeremy Horton.
His Lievtenant, Tho. Browne.
His Enfigne, Ed. Greene.
Serjeant Major, Owen Parry.
His Lievtenant, Ed. Browne.
His Enfine, Rob. Hughes.
Firft Captain, Vincent Calmady.
  his Lievtenant, Edward Tyrer.
  his Enfigne, Richard Bland.
Second Captain, Robert Long.
  his Lievtenant, Tho. Allanby.
  his Enfigne, Roger Moore.

Third Captain, Henry Carew.
  his Lievtenant, Charles Holcroft.
  his Enfigne, William Heyden.
Fourth Captain, Henry Skipwith.
  his Lievtenant, Jo. Ivey.
  his Enfigne, Oliver St. John.
Fifth Cap. of Fire-Locks, Elias Struice.
  his Lievtenant, Ed. Gray.
  his Enfigne, Tho. Barber.

Second Colonell, Lord Kerry.
  his Lievtenant, Robert Hamond.
  his Enfigne, Richard Bagot.

---

[166] Afterwards Lord Protector. From this entry it is evident that Oliver Cromwell, before being a colonel of horfe, had held a commiffion in a foot regiment. The earlieft copy of this lift of "Field Officers for the Irifh Expedition" that I have feen is a broadfide in the Britifh Mufeum, (669. f. 6). "London Printed for Edward Paxton, June 11, 1642." See further, in proof of Oliver Cromwell once having been a foot foldier, in *Notes and Queries*, Second Series, vol. xii. p. 285.

[*IRISH EXPEDITION.*]

Lievtenant Colonell, Henry Shelley.
  his Lievtenant, Jo. Ramsford.
  his Enſigne, Jo. Aſhfield.
Sergeant Major, Daniel Goodrick.
  his Lievtenant, Geo. Lower.
  his Enſigne, Charles Blount.
Firſt Captain, Charles Dawſon.
  his Lievtenant, Philip Meautas.
  his Enſigne, Jacob Stringer.
Second Captain, Herbert Blankchard.
  his Lievtenant, Morgan Tinney.
  his Enſigne, Chriſtoph. Chudleigh.
Third cap. Agmondiſham Murſchamp.
  his Lievtenant, Will. Dothwait.
  his Enſigne, Gervaſe Brach.
Fourth Captain, Paul Wats.
  his Lievtenant, Andr. Manwarring.
  his Enſigne, Tho. Barriffe.
Fifth Capt. for Firelocks, Wil. Lower.
  his Lievtenant, . . . Redman.
  his Enſigne, Jo. Raymond.

Third Colonell, Tho. Ballard.
  his Lievtenant, Tho. Grover.
  his Enſigne, Leonard Morton.

Lievtenant Colonell, Sir Ed. Denny.
  his Lievtenant, Ed. Odingſells.
  his Enſigne, William Garfoot.
Sergeant Major, Francis Martin.
  his Lievtenant, Rob. Noyce.
  his Enſigne, Jo. Hardy.
Firſt Captain, Captain Primroſe.
  his Lievtenant, Edward Norbury.
  his Enſigne, William Fowlis.
Second Captain, Edward Allen.
  his Lievtenant, Fran. Bowyer.
  his Enſigne, Robert Goodwin.
Third Captain, Fran. Fook.
  his Lievtenant, Tho. Nayerne.
  his Enſigne, Hen. Higgins.
Fourth Captain, Thomas Middleton.
  his Lievtenant, Jo. Lookar.
  his Enſigne, Charles Parker.
Fifth Captain for Firelocks, Pet. Nurford.
  his Lievtenant, Robert Davis.
  his Enſigne, Hen. Cope.

Fourth Colonell, Charles Eſſex.
  his Lievtenant, Fran. Hall.
  his Enſigne, Jo. Shipman.
Lievt. Col. Adam Cunningham.
  his Lievtenant, Peter Criſpe.
  his Enſigne, Leonard Hawkins.
Sergeant Major, Tho. Ogle.

[IRISH EXPEDITION.]

his Lievtenant, James Webb.
his Enfigne, Richard Ofborne.
Firſt Captain, William Roberts.
his Lievtenant, Ambrofe Tindall.
his Enfigne, Jo. Watkins.
Second Captain, George Narrow.
his Lievtenant, Edward Barnwell.
his Enfigne, Tho. Paramour.
Third Captain, Conſtance Ferrer.
his Lievtenant, William Hewet.
his Enfigne, Jo. Hemings.
Fourth Captain, Sam. Loftus.
his Lievtenant, James Barrell.
his Enfigne, Fran. Butler.
Fifth Cap. for Firelocks, John Jinkins.
his Lievtenant, Bartho. Elecot.
his Enfigne, Mr. Wayte.

Fifth Colonell, William Bamfield.
his Captain, Sam. Price.
his Enfigne, ... Cafworth.

Lievtenant Colonell, ... Wagſtaffe.
his Lievtenant, Tho. Coleby.
his Enfigne, Robert Nelfon.
Sergeant Major, George Hutchinfon.
his Lieutenant, Jo. Minſhaw.
his Enfign, William Bourcher.
Firſt Captain, Jo. Bainfield.
his Lievtenant, Richard Bingley.
his Enfigne, Ralph Garts.
Second Captain, Horatio Carey.
his Lievtenant, Allen Povey.
his Enfigne, Humfrey Burton.
Third Captain, Robert Baker.
his Lievtenant, Michael Bland.
his Enfigne, Jo. Rofe.
Fourth Captain, Chriſtoph. Burgh.
his Lievtenant, Tho. Hoare.
his Enfigne, Samuel Manaton.
Fifth Cap. for Firelocks, Rich. Benfon.
his Lievtenant, Tho. Latimer.
his Enfigne, Jo. Browne.

APPENDIX.

APPENDIX.

I.

The Names of all the Collonels, Lieutenant Collonels, Sergeant Majors, Captains, Lieutenants, Enſignes, Preachers, Chirurgeons, Quarter Maſters, Provoſt Marſhals under his Excellency the EARL OF NORTHUMBERLAND, *Captain General for this Expedition.* 1640. *Taken according to the Muſter Roll after the Armies Retreat from Newcaſtle into Yorkſhire.*

[RUSHWORTH's *Hiſtorical Collections*, Vol. II. Pt. II. p. 1243.]

1.

IS Excellency Algernon Earl of Northumberland, Captain General.
William Aſhburnham, Lieutenant Collonel.
Thomas Latham, Sergeant Major.

Captains.	
Charles Lloyde.	Jonathan Atkins.
Henry Waſhington.[167]	Richard Dowſe.
	Giles Porter.
	James Chudley.

---

[167] Henry Waſhington was the only ſurviving ſon of Sir Wm. Waſhington, Kt. (of the ancient family of Sulgrave, co. Northampton), of Packington,

[APPENDIX.]

George Herne.
John Edwards.

Lieutenants.

Guy Molefworth.
Lewis Gifford.
John Tooley.
Henry Chayton.
William Moore.
William Palmer.
Barnaby Bradford.
Edward Landen.
Thomas Wylde.
Nathaniel Dillon.
Triftram Fenwicke.
Roger Larrimore.

Enfignes.

John Newton.
William Wentworth.
Thomas Parrimore.

Stephen Dawfon.
Charles Fofter.
Henry Miller.
Robert Brandling.
Robert Marfh.
Edward Jackfon.
John Hilderfon.
John Salkeld.
David Farrington.

Preacher.

Mr. William Cox.

Chirurgeon.

Laurence Lowe.

Quarter-mafter.

Thomas Sandford.

Provoft Marfhal.

James Jeftres.

The Right Honourable Edward Lord Vifcount Conway,[168] Captain General of the Horfe, confifting of 35 Troops already raifed.

---

co. Leicefter, and Ifleworth, co. Middlefex, by Anne, daughter of Sir George Villiers of Brokefby, co. Leicefter, Kt. and half-fifter of George, firft Duke of Buckingham. He was born in 1615. He ferved through all the Civil Wars on the loyal fide, and rofe to the rank of colonel. He refigned the reverfion of the Cuftomer's place at Gravefend, 28 December, 1663, and died fhortly after, leaving 4 daughters and co-heirs by Elizabeth his wife, daughter of Sir John Pakington, Kt. and Bart., who remarried Samuel Sandys of Omberfley, Efq.

[168] Edward Conway, fecond Vifcount, fon and heir of Edward Conway, the firft Vifcount. Succeeded, 1630. Died, 1655.

[*APPENDIX.*]

II.

Earl of Newport, Collonel.
George Moncke,[169] Lieutenant Coll.
Henry Warren, Sergeant Major.

Captains.

Robert Crofts.
Thomas Shelton.
John Stradling.
Posthumus Kirton.
William Cope.
Henry Vanpeere.
Cashea Burrowes.

Lieutenants.

George Lower.
Arthur Moncke.
Thomas Vaughan.
Edmund Goffe.
George Cooke.
John Hoskins.
John Weekes.
James Gardiner.
Owen Owens.
Daniel Don.

Ensignes.

John Hamond.
Richard Legg.
John Fox.
John Blunt.
Thomas Paramore.
Montague Sanderson.
John Lutterell.
John Washington.
Edward Armory.
Robert Bonny.

Preacher.

Higham Gibbs.

Chirurgeon.

Anthony Coquinx.

Quarter-master.

George Lawdy.

Provost.

John Parker.

III.

Sir Jacob Ashley, Collonel.
Sir Nicholas Selwin, Lieutenant Collonel.
Bernard Ashley, Sergeant Major.

Captains.

Sr William Vudall.
Robert Townsend.

---

[169] Born at Potheridge, co. Devon, 6 Dec. 1608. Served on the Royal side until taken prisoner at Nantwich, 25 Jan. 1643-4. Afterwards served the Parliament, and in course of time brought about the Restoration. Created Duke of Albemarle 7 July, 1660. Died 3 Jan. 1669-70.

[*APPENDIX.*]

James Baynton.
William Bellowes.
Robert Rufhell.
Edward Aftley.
..... St. Johns.

Lieutenants.

William Lower.
Michael Bedolph.
Edward Fowles.
George Slatford.
Deverex Gibbons.
John Haflewood.
Ifaac Cobb.
Theodore Paleologus.
Thomas Colbie.
Henry Somerfter.

Enfignes.

Edward Courtney.
Bray Knight.
Francis Gay.
Walter Neal.
Peregrine Tafburgh.
Hugh Pomeroy.
Edward Nelfon.
Charles Thompfon.
..... Oxford.
George Fuller.

Preacher.

John Kowland.

Chirurgeon.

John Auftin.

Quarter-Mafter.

..... Rawlins.

Provoft-Marfhal.

Paul Knight.

IV.

George Goring, Collonel.
Thomas Kirke, Lieutenant Coll.
Richard Willis, Sergeant Major.

Captains.

Henry Sully.
William Preddocks.
Andrew Menns.
Charles Gerrard.
Edward Gray.
Richard Elliot.
Thomas Danil.

Lieutenants.

Richard Dowes.
William Langon.
William Swan.
Henry Cooke.
John Marly.
Thomas Throgmorton.
Robert Noyfe.
Francis Grover.
Daniel More.
Phillip Honywood.

Enfignes.

Richard Lovellis.

[*APPENDIX.*] 77

Henry Crompton.
. . . . . Warren.
John Terwhit.[170]
John Millard.
John Barbridge.
Francis Lifle.
Ralph Brandling.
Jofeph Brand.
Arthur Chaune.

Preacher.

Richard Lloyde.

Chirurgeon.

. . . . .

Quarter Mafter.

Ben. Lawerowyes.

Provoft Marfhal.

Thomas Broxley.

v.

The Lord Vifcount Grandifon, Collonel.
Thomas Ballard, Lieutenant Coll.
Henry Sibthorpe, Sergeant Major.

Captains.

William Pretty.

Francis Smith.
Edward Villars.
Thomas Ellis.
George Lifle.
Edward Urney.
John Boyes.

Lieutenants.

Thomas Browne.
William Alford.
John Malorye.
William Smith.
Robert Wiltfhire.
Robert Wynd.
John Eaton.
Daniel Broughton.
Francis Gaudy.
Phillip Ballard.

Enfignes.

John Bennet.
John Carter.
Hugh Juftice.
Henry Crooker.
Henry Payton.
Ralph Sparkes.
Henry Marfhin.
John Cooney.
John Walters.

Preacher.

Thomas Kent.

---

[170] John, fixth fon of Robert Tyrwhitt of Cameringham, co. Lincoln, and his wife Anne Baffet.

[APPENDIX.]

Chirurgeon.

John Earnleffe.

Quarter Mafter.

Phillip Cooke.

Provoft Marfhal.

Marmaduke Collins.

VI.

David Earl of Barrimore, Coll.
Garret Barry, Lieutenant Coll.
James Ufher, Sergeant Major.

Captains.

Thomas Trafford.
John Fitzgerald.
Miles Power.
Henry Obrian.
George White.
Charles Henife.
Garret Parfell.

Lieutenants.

Daniel Boulton.
David Barry.
Richard Greatrix.
Thomas Pheafant.
Lodowicke Price.
Samuel Wright.
William Wefton.
John Ruffell.
Charles Stepkin.
Richard Barry.

Enfignes.

William Barry.
Phillip Barry.
James Dallochin.
John Barry.
Nicholas Barry.
Neptune Howard.
James Bladwell.
William Norcott.
Robert Rofington.
William Tomkins.

Preacher.

John Rocke.

Chirurgeon.

Charles Oxenbridge.

Quarter Mafter.

Thomas Owens.

Provoft-Marfhall.

John Baldwin.

VII.

Arthur Afhton, Collonel.
Richard Bole, Lieutenant Coll.
Robert Cogningefby, Sergeant
  Major.

Captains.

Ifaac Lukine.
Richard Bradfhaw.
Henry Keyes.

[*APPENDIX.*]

Henry Thomas.
Thomas Leighton.
William Courtney.
James Thomson.

Lieutenants.

Thomas Minn.
William Keeling.
Richard Spoore.
William Rofton.
John Skipwith.
Charles Hales.
Celeftine Bingham.
Vul . . . Wright.
Nathaniel Moyle.
Stafford Sherborne.

Enfignes.

Francis Afton.
Robert Bowles.
Phillip Lowes.
Robert Smith.
John Atkins.
James Browne.
Robert Nelfon.
George Leigh.
Richard Leigh.
John Mynne.

Preacher.

Henry Jones.

Chirurgeon.

. . . . .

Quarter Mafter.

Lodowick Burwick.

Provoft Marfhal.

Tho. Goubourne.

VIII.

Henry Wentworth, Collonel.
Henry Waite, Lieutenant Coll.
William Brockett, Serg. Major.

Captains.

Sir Chriftopher Abdey.
William Roberts.
Owen Parry.
John Holman.
Broichel Lloyd.
Henry Fotherfby.

Lieutenants.

Francis Kanyer.
Frederick Windfor.
Francis Boyer.
Hugh Williams.
Jofeph Bamfeild.
Robert Bingham.
Gilbert Wheathill.
John Higham.
Thomas Stanbury.
Robert Rookes.

Enfignes.

Edward Roberts.
Ifaac Throughton.

[*APPENDIX.*]

John Thomas.
Francis Smithwick.
Humfrey Standburgh.
William Lewis.
Phillip Norris.
Edmond Brockett.
James Esline.
Robert Herne.

Preacher.

Mr. Matthew Whitley.

Chirurgeon.

Edward Hales.

Quarter Master.

William Bury.

Provost Marshall.

John Hodson.

IX.

Sir Thomas Glenham, Collonel.
Sir John Pawlett, Lieutenant Col.
Sir John Beaumont, Serg. Major.

Captains.

Robert Kirbie.
Robert Pirkins.
George Whither.
. . . . . Waldgrave.
Nicholas Codrington.
Robert Mynn.
Thomas Dymock.

Lieutenants.

John Waldgrave.
William Pawlett.
William Molineux.
William Greene.
Jacob Stringer.
Thomas Ward.
James Bassett.
Richard Norwood.
William Neve.

Ensignes.

Edward Pereont.
Thomas Pawlett.
John Beamont.
Theodore Delastey.
Thomas Sanders.
Hugh Gerrard.
Francis Godfrey.
Arthur Ward.
Henry Reyley.

Preacher.

. . . . .

Chirurgeon.

. . . . . . Palmer.

Quarter Master.

William Moore.

Provost Marshal.

William Swaine.

[*APPENDIX.*] 81

X.

Sir John Mirick, Collonel.
Thomas Carne, Lieutenant Coll.
William Davis, Sergeant Major.

Captains.

Robert Broughton.
Edward Seymore.
Thomas Button.
William Herbert.
David Hide.
Charles Skrumſhaw.
William May.

Lieutenants.

Thomas Langham.
William Mathews.
John Butler.
Ambroſe Tindall.
John Edwards.
William Mintridge.
..... Braſſe.
..... Waldwine.
George Betts.
John Lloyd.

Enſignes.

..... Auberry.
John Luther.
William Owen.
Thomas Smith.
Thomas Cardinall.
Gelly Merick.

Miles Button.
Thomas Milſhaw.
..... Woods.
Thomas Thwaytes.

Preacher.

Dr. Edward Alcaron.

Chirurgeon.

. . . . .

Quarter Maſter.

Henry Biſhop.

Provoſt Marſhal.

Iſaac Chaliſe.

XI.

Sir Thomas Culpepper, Collonel.
Richard Gibſon, Lieutenant Coll.
Robert Turvill, Sergeant Major.

Captains.

Walter Owen.
Lewis Lewkner.
Rowland Sleger.
Henry Boyer.
Francis Cooke.
Richard Thurland.
Samuel Payton.

Lieutenants.

Daniel Nicholls

[APPENDIX.]

Compton Evers.
John Sherman.
Henry Ugall.
William Mohun.
Edward Louch.
Richard Parker.
Anthony Bufhell.
Anthony Thorpe.
Richard Carter.

Enfignes.

Nicholas Lidcott.
Thomas Lyfter.
John Chyne.
Robert Goodwine.
Peter Brewnett.
John Steed.
Lionell Beecher.
..... Bowdon.
William Waldron.
John Scanderith.

Preacher.

Mr. Edward Langford.

Chirurgeon.

. . . . .

Quarter Mafter.

William Wheeler.

Provoft-Marfhal.

..... Turner.

XII.

Sir Charles Vavafor, Collonel.
..... Howard, Lieutenant Coll.
..... Appleyard, Sergeant Major.

Captains.

..... Bafcarvill.
..... Winde.
..... Scudamore.
..... Therneton.
..... Pate.
..... Kinfman.
..... Doneill.

Lieutenants.

Thomas Bafcarvell.
William Evert.
Phillip Hutton.
Edward Dymmocke.
Nathaniel Smith.
James Marwood.
John Griffith.
Edward Molworth.
Jeremy Cheviers.
George Mafters.

Enfignes.

William Blakiftone.
Averoy Maleroy.
Henry Chrifwell.
Richard Mafon.
Samuel Mallowes.

[*APPENDIX.*] 83

Thomas Chapline.
William Carre.
Edward Cropley.
John Holland.
Giles Palmer.

Preacher.

Mr. Thompſon.

Chirurgeon.

. . . . Bennett.

Quarter Maſter.

Rolland Davis.

Provoſt Marſhal.

William Powell.

XIII.

William Vavafor, Collonel.
Nicholas Mynne, Lieutenant Col.
Thomas Pagett, Sergeant Major.

Captains.

Charles Gillmore.
Edward Brett.
William Bedingfeild.
Lancelot Houltby.
. . . . . Nicholls.
Francis Layton.
Henry Ferries.

Lieutenants.

Robert Griffith.

Ralph King.
Francis Cowgrave.
Owen Collugno.
Nicholas Hughes.
Francis Mills.
John Wren.
Robert Nicholas.
Arthur Grant.
Arthur Lowe.

Enſignes.

Edward Cheſter.
. . . . Finch.
Henry Baggett.
Thomas Audey.
Charles Fox.
George Drewell.
Fenix Wilſon.
Benjamin Brett.
John Jefford.
Robert Hugganes.

Preacher.

Mr. Chriſtian Sherwood.

Chirurgeon.

Trinity Langley.

Quarter Maſter.

Humf. Farrew.

Provoſt Marſhal.

. . . . .

XIV.

..... Lunsford,[171] Collonel.
Hen. Lunsford, Lieutenant Col.
..... Powell, Sergeant Major.

Captains.

..... Dillon.
Herbert Lunsford.
Francis Martin.
Thomas Cupper.
Hugh Pomeroy.
Edward Powell.
Edward Hippesley.

Lieutenants.

John Iremonger.
Thomas Owen.
John Sanbedge.

Thomas Carrow.
Ralph Lilley.
Allen Povey.
Poynton Castillion.
Phillip Chalwell.
Edward Hulstone.
William Cheney.

Ensignes.

Titus Layton.
Robert Skerrew.
Edward Fowles.
John Meredith.
Pilemon Sanders.
William Atkins.
William Bellow.
Greevile Cary.
John Cole.

---

[171] Sir Thomas Lunsford, Kt., son of Thomas Lunsford of Wilegh, co. Sussex, by his wife Katherine, daughter of Sir Thomas Fludd of Milgate, co. Kent, sister to Dr. Robert Fludd, *alias* de Fluctibus the Mystic. Absurd stories were current during the war, representing Sir Thomas as a cannibal, one who delighted in eating the flesh of babies. In one of the satirical hymns that were current we find this petition:—

"From Fielding and from Vavasour,
   Both ill-affected men;
From Lunsford eke deliver us,
   That eateth up childeren."—*Rump Songs,* I. 65.

Sir Walter Scott quotes in *Woodstock* (chap. xx.) a verse from a contemporary song which sets forth how

"The post who came from Coventry,
   Riding on a red rocket,
Did tidings tell, how Lunsford fell,
   A child's hand in his pocket."

See also *Hudibras,* Part III. Canto II. line 1112.

Preacher.

. . . .

Chirurgeon.

. . . . .

Quarter Master.
Anth. Witherings.

Provost-Marshal.
Elias Hickmar.

XV.

Sir William Ogle, Collonel.
Brutus Bucke, Lieutenant Coll.
Richard Lawdey, Sergeant Major.

Captains.

Constance Ferrer.
Edward Drury.
Edward Andrews.
Henry Ventris.
Robert Sandes.
Richard Power.
Conyer Griffen.

Lieutenants.

. . . . . Fleetwood.
Thomas Laward.
Peter Gleane.
Cornelius Ragan.
George Lambert.
Thomas Bennett.

Charles Kirke.
Edward Hackluyt.
Thomas King.
Francis Moore.

Ensignes.

Thomas Symoure.
Edward Ogle.
. . . . . Banard.
Edward Maylard.
Hugh Leigh.
John Waite.
William Andrewes.
Gerrard Ogle.
Hugh Gue.
Robert Bacon.

Preacher.

Mr. John Phillips.

Chirurgeon.

Henry Barker.

Quarter Master.

George Lisle.

Provost Marshal.

Thomas Bragge.

XVI.

James, Marquis of Hamilton, Coll.
Edward Feilding, Lieutenant Coll.
John Berry, Sergeant Major.

[*APPENDIX.*]

Captains.

William Monnings.
Paul Smith.
Francis Langley.
Jervas Paine.
Howard St. Johns.
Peter Walthall.
Anthony Greene.
Charles Dawſon.
Thomas Boſome.

Lieutenants.

Moſes Treadwell.
Emanuel Neale.
William Denn.
William Tuke.
William Gualter.
George Rouſe.
Godard Pemberton.
Thomas Throughwood.
George Little.
Henry Bowerman.
Henry Peto.
John Wolverſtone.
Robert Watham.

Enſignes.

Bennet Prior.
Henry Peters.
Richard Cooke.
Thomas Pergent.
William Reevs.
Walter Price.
Anthony Williams.

John Prenton.
Thomas Beſt.
Francis Willier.
Thomas Carde
..... Rogers.
William Lane.

Preacher.

Mr. Deight.

Chirurgeon.

Richard Smith.

Quarter Maſter.

Jo. Daniell.

Provoſt Marſhal.

Henry Fiſher.

XVII.

Sir Nicholas Biron, Collonel.
.... Lieutenant Coll.
Edward Aldrich, Sergeant Major.

Captains.

John Watts.
Thomas Sherley.
John Middleton.
Abraham Shipman.
James Morgan.
Roger Mollineux.
Sheerly Shilling.
Herculus Huncks.
William Paterſon.

[*APPENDIX.*] 87

Lieutenants.

Francis Stradling.
Daniel Trever.
Thomas Rush.
John Marshall.
Thomas Brumley.
John Carnocke.
Ralph Freeman.
John Chonnocke.
Edward Watts.
Ithiell Luch.
Thomas Garrett.

Ensignes.

Lambert Colield.
Richard Bond.
Michael Bland.
John Exton.
John Shipman.
Daniel Redman.
Christopher Elfing.
John Elrington.
George Hartrigg.
Tho. May.
Nicholas Watson.
William Winter.

Preacher.

. . . . .

Chirurgeon.

. . . . .

Quarter Master.

Henry Bluder.

Provost Marshal.

John Fletcher.

XVIII.

Sir James Hamilton, Collonel.
John Slaughter, Lieutenant Coll.
Francis Story, Sergeant Major.

Captains.

Thomas Dabscoate.
Horatio Carew.
Richard Munington.
Thomas Gardiner.
Thomas Cornewallis.
Bullen Erreny.
Anthony Brockett.
Thomas Gifford.
Thomas Bushell.

Lieutenants.

Thomas Rockwood.
William Balyes.
Roger May.
John Andrewes.
John Grove.
Duke Calton.
William Corney.
Thomas Townsend.
Humfry Corey.
John Goodrich.
Francis Poore.
Thomas Bancks.

88 [*APPENDIX.*]

Enſignes.
John Blunt.
John Heaflewood.
Thomas Shelton.
William Stratford.
George Burwell.
Iſaac Wally.
John Food.
Thomas Leigh.
Robert Bayles.
John Lycent.
Edward Purpitt.
John Jervas.

Preacher.
Mr. Henry Miller.

Chirurgeon.
. . . . .

Quarter Maſter.
Will. Dethick.

Provoſt Marſhal.
Will. Richardſon.

XIX.

Sir Jo. Douglefs, Collonel.
Sir Mathew Carry, Lieuten. Coll.
Arthur Baſſet, Sergeant Major.

Captains.
Sir John le Hunt.
Charles Ventreſs.
Edward Kingſtone.
Thomas Middleton.
John Barſey.
James Powell.
Robert Burghill.
Nicholas Parker.
George Windham.

Lieutenants.
Robert Gandey.
Roger Hiddon.
Samuel Keviſon.
Robert Davis.
Thomas Ferrors.
Robert Hamlon.
William Gamblin.
William Roſs.
James Carwardine.
Thomas Andrewes.
Thomas Draper.
Robert Davyes.

Enſignes.
Thomas Kingſtone.
Silvanus Keyghtley.
William Codrington.
Mich. Doughty.
Humfrey Cornwall.
Richard Naupham.
George Carew.
Thomas Carleton.
Hugh Lovelace.
Thomas Rookes.
Edward Knightly.
Thomas Coote.

[*APPENDIX.*]

Preacher.

Mr. Humfry Sloconil.

Chirurgeon.

Clodius Adney.

Quarter Mafter.

Robert Juns.

Provoft Marfhal.

Richard Read.

xx.

Jerom Brett, Collonel.
Sir Vivian Molineux, Lieutenant Collonel.
William Gibbs, Sergeant Major.

Captains.

Thomas Brett.
Bartholomew Jukes.
Stephen Hawkins.
George Leake.
Thomas Pettus.
Henry Huddlefton.
John Godfrey.
Digory Collins.
Humfry Nichols.

Lieutenants.

John Fifher.
William Simpfon.
John Glaffington.

Francis Hooke.
Robert Benbricke.
John Palmer.
John Clifton.
Daniel Robinfon.
Nicholas Barnet.
Nicholas Browne.
Thomas Mollineaux.
Giles Bafkervill.

Enfignes.

Ambrofe Jenings.
Poole Turvill.
Norrice Jepfon.
Thomas Hunt.
Ifaac Shawbury.
Francis Bret.
Thomas Birke.
Francis Cobb.
John Hunt.
Roger Bendifh.
William Draper.

Preacher.

John Weld.

Chirurgeon.

. . . . .

Quarter Mafter.

Will. Bellamy.

Provoft Marfhal.

John Vittell.

XXI.

Francis Hamond, Collonel.
Robert Hamond, Lieutenant Col.
John Gifford, Sergeant Major.

Captains.

Mathew Gray.
Edward Hamond.
John Bayley.
Arthur Roberts.
James Ogle.
Robert Afcough.
Jeremy Manwood.
Benjamin Eldred.
Henry Mathews.

Lieutenants.

Roger Burges.
Thomas Conifby.
Nicholas Deane.
John Worfop.
Daniel Goldfmith.
Francis Whitney.
Robert Scott.
George Warfon.
Edward Tyerer.
William Fifher.
Chriftopher Crowe.
Mathew Plowman.

Enfignes.

James Tooke.
Richard Travers.
. . . . . Walton.
Edward Gray.
Thomas Swinford.
Henry Blundell.
Ralph Murrian.
Thomas Walkington.
John Philpot.
Henry Echlyn.
. . . . . Plomer.
John Fitz James.

Preacher.

Henry Pike.

Chirurgeon.

. . . . .

Quarter Mafter.

Ferdinando Gray.

Provoft Marfhal.

Nicholas Knot.

XXII.

Richard Feilding, Collonel.
Francis Tirwhit, Lieutenant Coll.
Anthony Thelwall, Sergeant Major.

Captains.

Francis Tirringham.
John Talbot.
Thomas Collins.

[*APPENDIX.*]

Toby Bowes.
Edward Tirwhit.
William Rolson.
Robert Appleton.
John Fox.
Robert Barker.

Lieutenants.

Richard Oxenden.
Denny Purvey.
George Oakes.
Salathiel Baxter.
Thomas Hill.
John Windfeild.
John Errington.
Edward Vincent.
George Foord.
John Cratroft.
John Sutton.

Ensignes.

Francis Rogers.
Henry Garfeild.

Richard Francis.
Edward Bray.
Henry Hatcher.
John Tirwhit.
Foulke Woodroffe.
Edward Disney.
Charles Persall.
Robert Ruston.
. . . . . . Cosworth.

Preacher.

William Beare.

Chirurgeon.

. . . . .

Quarter Master.

Walter Harcourt.

Provost Marshal.

Christopher Woodman.

[APPENDIX.]

II.

A Lift of fuch Englifh and Scotch Commanders, as Captains, Lievtenants, and Enfignes, and Sergeants, as have left their command under the Prince of Orange, *from his leager at Rhineberk, with the names of each Captain's Garrifon.*

[The following lift exifts as a broadfide among the King's Pamphlets in he Britifh Mufeum. If not unique, it is of a high degree of rarity. The date of its publication is probably fixed within a few days by a manufcript memorandum of the collector, who records that he acquired it "Aug. 12, 1642." After the name of Serjeant Philpot—that is, at the bottom of the firft column in the original—there is written, "Thefe are for the King's fervices." Whether this refers to the names in that column only, or to the whole lift, may be a matter of doubt.]

English.

At the Maiden Toun of Dort.

Captaine Booth.
Captaine Ogle.
Lievtenant Winter.
Lievtenant Ringrofe.
Lievtenant Johnfon.
Enfigne Preftwood.
Serjeant Honywood.
Serjeant Wifeman.

At Bullduke.

Captaine Floyd.
Lievtenant Waters.
Serjeant Fofter.

At Hufdon.

Captaine Morgan.
Lievtenant Morgan.
Enfigne White.
Enfigne Cockin.
Serjeant Weft.
Serjeant Wells.

At Nimingham.

Captaine Charles Morgan.
Enfigne Jones.
Enfigne Rowland.
Serjeant Wats.

[*APPENDIX.*]

At Bergen op Zoom.

Captaine Pollard.
Lievtenant Browne.
Lievtenant Roofe.
Enfigne Williams.
Serjeant Iackfon.

At Surrexfey.

Captaine Vanhuifh.
A Dutchman.
Serjeant Eeafon.

At Bumble.

Captaine Crelawny (*fic*).
Lievtenant Morgan.
Lievtenant Waller.
Serjeant Cox.

At Workecum.

Enfigne Strowd.
Enfigne Carre.
Enfigne Maidftone.

At Gittermberk.

Captaine Southcot.
Lievtenant Prat.
Enfigne Vandowfe.
A Dutchman.
Serjeant Fox.

At Girkcum.

Captaine Staunton.
Captaine Serjeant.
Lievtenant Horfey.
Lievtenant Flood.
Enfigne Maddocke.
Serjeant Philpot.

SCOTCH.

At Rotterdam.

Captaine Stewart.
Captaine Douglas.
Lievtenant Mounfon.
Lievtenant Angel.
Enfigne Stewart.
Enfigne Culveer.
Serjeant Dafhfield.
Quarter-mafter Hayfe.

At Flufhing.

Captaine Belford.
Captaine Sowfe.

Enfigne Vicceers.
Serjeant Rifey.

At Middleborough.

Captaine Polwheele.
Serjeant Douglas.
Lievtenant Parree.
Lievtenant Voyfey.
Enfigne Bellew.
Serjeant Benfon.

At Amfterdam.

Captaine Ramfey.

94   [APPENDIX.]

Lievtenant Belford.
Lievtenant Murrey.
Enſigne Douglas.
Enſigne Skut.
Enſigne Vaux.
Enſigne Fiddler.

At the Brill.

Captaine Hamilton.

Serjeant Sowton.
Serjeant Marſh.
Serjeant Prieſt.
Serjeant Vpton.

At Iſendike.

Lievtenant Maio.
Lievtenant Gey.

I have intellegence likewiſe that diverſe Captaines and officers under the command of Colonel Gage, in Flanders, do intend to meet at Dunkirke, if not the Collonel himſelf.

London, printed for Robert Wood, 1642.

III.

Priſoners of warre taken in Nableſby field, June 14th, 1645, in Com. Northton.

[*The Hiſtory of Naſeby*, by Rev. John Maſtin, Cambridge, 1792, p. 154. Taken from " A manuſcript in the poſſeſſion of Sir Thomas Cave, Bart." Rushworth's *Hiſt. Coll.* part iv. vol. i. p. 46, contains a ſimilar liſt, but abounding even more than the one here given with clerical and printers' errors.]

Col. Sr Riſe Page.
Theophilus Gilby, Col.
Lieut. Col. Woodhouſe.
Lieut. Col. Lawſon.
Lieut. Col. Burys.
Lieut. Col. Thornton.
Maior Bryin.
Maior Sr William Bridge.
Maior Pue.

Maior Moore.
Maior Whitford.
Maior Den.
Maior Hooker.
Maior Riſely, of horſe.
Cap. Thornton, of horſe.
Cap. Shafty, of horſe.
Cap. Lieut. Carnaby, of horſe.
Cap. Lieut. Lambton, of horſe.

[*APPENDIX.*]

Officers of the King's Life Guards, Foote.

Cap. Fox.
Cap. Lewens.
Cap. Flyer.
Cap. Benton.
Cap. Barby.
Cap. Lieut. Waller.
Lieut. Mewfey.

Lieut. Brown.
Enfigne Chamberlain.
Enfigne Porter.
Enfigne Berkenhead.
Enfigne Ingolfby.
Enfigne Moufehall.

Life Guard of Horse.

Captain Mufon, Reformado.

Officers of the Duke of York's Regiment.

Cap. Fitzmorris.
Cap. Widnam.
Cap. Hill.
Cap. Dier.
Cap. Lieut. Hawkfworth.
Lieut. Roffey.

Lieut. Curlys.
Ryley.
Enfigne Bennet.
Rofley.
Young.
Bradfhaw.

Prince Rupert's Regiment of Horse.

Lieut. Fryeer.

Officers in Prince Maurice's Life Guard of Horse.

Cap. Garret.
Cap. Tempeft.

Lieut. Baxter.
Quarter-mafter Simpfon.

Officers of the Lord Astley's Regiment of Foote.

Cap. Walley.
Cap. Jackfon.
Cap. Wright.
Cap. Fowler.

Cap. Bakerfield, Reformado.
Enfigne Ridley.
Enfigne Rowland.
Bennet Corpale of the field.

Officers of Sir Barnard's Regiment of Foote.

Cap. Hoare.
Fisher.
Lieut. Weller.
Simons.
Smith.

Lieut. Harden.
Ensigne Chester.
Homes.
Symons.

Of Col. Appleyard's Regiment of Foote.

Cap. Triwhit.
Masters.
Sanderson.
Hubbart.

Lieut. Middleton.
Thompson.
Lewen.
Baker.

Of Col. Bagott's Regiment of Foote.

Cap. Diot.
Glazier.
Lieut. Ward.
Baggeley.
Cowper, Refor.

Ensigne Sharpe.
Blencarne.
Emmins.
Thomas.

Of Col. Sir John Pawlet's Regiment of Foote.

Cap. Mason.
Lieut. Birkwhit.
Wynn.
Kirkman.
Bradford.
Burling.

Ensigne Yate.
Glascock.
Hutchins.
Rise.
Cooke.

Of Col. Gerrard's Regiment of Foote.

Maior Bishop.
Cap. Booth.

Ensigne Blancy.
Perrin.

[*APPENDIX.*] 97

Of Col. Page's Regiment of Foote.

Col. Page.
Lieut. Col. Lawson.
Maior Sir Wm. Bridges.
Cap. Etherington.
 Norton.
 Pearson.
 Carrington.
 Beneson.
 Simpson.
Lieut. Vertaine.

Lieut. Egleton.
 Pilkinton.
 Bates.
 Royndtree.
 Flexney.
 Ballard.
 Roberts.
Ensigne Etherington.
 Lyng.
 Scot.

Of Col. Lyle's Regiment of Foote.

Lieut. Col. Littleton.
Maior Fowler.
Cap. Skirrough.
 Whitgreen.
 Littleton.

Cap. Pocklington.
Lieut. Carter.
Ensigne Turpin.
 Littleton.

Of Col. St. George's Regiment of Foot.

Maior Whitmore.
Cap. Owens.
 Lawrens.
 Lawrens.
 Herne.

Lieut. Jones.
 Nassey.
 Jones.
 Jones.
Ensigne Fenn.

Of Col. Murrey's Regiment of Foote.

Maior Whitford.
Lieut. Sneyles.
 Griffise.

Ensigne Hygham.
 Cecil, Refor.

Of Col. Sir Bard's Regiment of Foote.

Cap. Lesley.
 Deuolet.

Cap. Lieut. Lawson.
Lieut. Fowler.

Lieut. Twifield. | Enfigne Dobyfon.
Windfor. | Fairbrother.

Of Col. Vaughan's Regiment of Horse.

Lieut. Col. Slaughter. | Cornet Edmonds.
Cap. Hofier. | Lieut. Billingley, Refor.
Lieut. Armftrong. | Quarter-mafter Nurfe.

Col. Broughton's Officers of Foote.

Cap. Lile. | Lieut. Duppey.
Cap. Polden. | Enfigne Vaughan.
Lieut. Darrenfield. | Pritchard.
Oliver. | Porter.
Morgan. |

Col. Tillard's Officers of Foote.

Cap. Church. | Enfigne Bowen.
Dykes. | Dillon.
Lieut. Bufbridge. | Loftus, fen.
Enfigne Harrifon. | Loftus, jun.

Col. Sir Fulk Hunks' Officers of Foote.

Lieut. Rewes. | Enfigne Smith.
Perren. |

Col. Lewsey's Officers of Foote.

Cap. Lieut. Parker. | Lieut. Cole.
Lieut. Johnfon. |

Befides thefe, 4500 more prifoners.

[*APPENDIX.*]

The Names of His Majefty's Houfehold-Servants now in the Marfhall's cuftody.

[The following immediately follows the preceding lift in Rufhworth. It is not given by Maftin.]

Mr. Howen, Page of his Majefty's Bed-Chamber.
Mr. Abbot, their Chamber-keeper.
One Sumpter man.
Four Footmen of his Majefties.
One Footman of Prince Maurice's.
Robert Markham, Yeoman of his Majefty's Chandry.
William Watfon, Porter at the Gate.
Roger Jellybrand, of his Majefty's Confectionary.
One Groom of the Chamber,
And One Chamber-keeper belonging to the Duke of Lenox.
Nicholas Johnfton, belonging to His Majefty's Groom Porter.
Walter Whife, belonging to his Majefty.
James Spanier, Victualler.
Francis Roffell.

More Prisoners of War.

Col. Bunkley, of Horfe.
Lieut. Col. Godfry.
Major More.
Captain King.
Lieutenant Griffin.
Lieutenant Nightingall.
Enfign Mufgrave.
Lieutenant Tench.
Thomas Mangainere, of the Prince's Troop.
Richard Addrings, Prince's Troop.
John Piffinch.

[*APPENDIX.*]

Joseph Bromehall.
Sir William Vahan.
Morgan Evans, the Queens Regiment.

IV.

A List of the Names of the Officers in Chief, of Foot and Horse, the Train of Artillery, and other Officers, under the command of his Excellency SIR THOMAS FAIRFAX; *as Colonels, Lieutenant-Colonels, Majors, and Captains, &c.*

[JOSHUA SPRIGG, *Anglia Rediviva,* Edit. 1647, p. 325; Edit. 1854, p. 327.]

GENERAL OFFICERS.

His Excellency Sir Thomas Fairfax, General.
Major General Skippon, Major General to the whole army.
Lieutenant General Cromwell, Lieutenant-General of Horse.
Lieutenat General Hammond, Lieutenant-General of the Ordnance.
Commissary-General Ireton, Commissary-General of the Horse.

THE TREASURERS AT WAR, VIZ.:

Sir John Wollaston.
Captain Blackwell, Deputy-Treasurer at Wars.

Commissary-General Stane, Commissary General of the Musters.
Major Watson, Scoutmaster General to the Army.
Quarter Master General Spencer, Quarter Master General of Foot (now Quarter Master General Gravesnor).
Quarter Master General Finchér, Quarter Master-General of Horse.
Captain Flemming } Adjutants-General of Horse.
Captain Evelyn }

[*APPENDIX.*]

Lieutenant-Colonel Gray, Adjutant-General of the Foot.
Captain Deane, Comptroller of the Ordnance.
John Rushworth, Esquire, Secretary to the General, and Com. of War.
Master Boles, Chaplain to the Army.
Colonel Pindar.
Harcourt Laighton.
Thomas Herbert. } Commissioners of Parliament residing in the Army.
Captain Potter, slain at Naseby (now Captain Vincent Potter, Esq.)
John Mills, Esquire, Judge Advocate.
Commissary Orpin, Commissary General of Victuals (now Commissary Cowling).
Captain Cook, Commissary General of Horse provisions, slain at Naseby (now Commissary Jones).
Master Richardson, Wagon-Master General.
Doctor Payne.
Dr. Stranhil (since Dr. French). } Physicians to the Army.
Master Web, Apothecary to the Army.
Master Winter, Chirurgeon General to the Army.
Captain Wykes, Marshal-General of Foot.
Captain Richard Lawrence, Marshal-General of Horse.
Mr. Fran. Child, Mark Master General of the Horse.
Master Robert Wolsey, Assistant to the Quarter Master General of Foot (wounded at Naseby).
Mr. James Standish, } Deputies to the Commissary General of Musters.
Mr. Richard Gerard,
Mr. Thomas Wragge, } Clerks to the Secretary.
Mr. William Clarke,
Mr. Richard Chadwell, } Messengers to the Army.
Mr. Constantine Heath,

For the Foot.

Sir Thomas Fairfax, Colonel: his own Company commanded by Captain Fortescue, since Captain Aidley.
Lieutenant Colonel Jackson.
Major Cook, died before Bristol; Captain Gooday now Major.
Captain Boyce.
Captain Musket.
Captain Maneste (dead).
Captain Wolfe.
Captain Highfield.
Captain White.
Captain Bland (since Captain Leigh).

Major-General Skippon.
Lieutenant-Colonel Frances, slain at Naseby.
Major Ashfield, now Lieutenant-Colonel.
Captain Samuel Clark, now Major.
Captain Streater.
Captain Harrison.
Captain John Clark.
Captain Bowen.
Captain Gibbon.
Captain Cobbet.
Captain Symonds.

Sir Hardress Waller, Colonel.
Lieutenant-Colonel Cottesworth, slain before Oxford, now Lieutenant-Colonel Salmon.
Major Smith.
Captain Howard.
Captain Waade.
Captain Hill, slain before Bristol, now Captain Aske.
Captain Gorges.
Captain Clark.

[*APPENDIX.*]

Captain Thomas.
Captain Hodden.

Colonel Hammond.
Lieutenant-Colonel Ewre.
Major Sanders.
Captain Difney.
Captain Chara.
Captain Smith.
Captain John Boyce.
Captain John Puckle.
Captain Stratton.
Captain Rolfe.

Colonel Harley.
Lieutenant-Colonel Pride.
Major Cowell.
Captain Goff.
Captain Gregfon, wounded at Berkeley.
Captain Sampfon, wounded at Bridgwater.
Captain Hinder, wounded at Briftol.
Captain Forgifon.
Captain Mafon.
Captain Lago.

Colonel Mountague, fince Colonel Lambert's.
Lieutenant-Colonel Grimes.
Major Kelfey, fince Major Rogers.
Captain Blethen.
Captain Nunney.
Captain Bifcoe.
Captain Rogers.
Captain Wilks, flain at Bafing, now Captain Cadwell.
Captain Thomas Difney.
Captain Sanders.

Colonel Lloyd, flain at Taunton, fince Colonel Herbert.

Lieutenant-Colonel Gray.
Major Read (now Lieutenant-Colonel,) wounded at Taunton, now Major Waade.
Captain Wilks, flain at Taunton.
Captain Gettins, died in Gloucefterfhire, now Captain Lundy, wounded at Berkeley.
Captain Wigfal, flain at Berkeley Caftle.
Captain Melvin, wounded at Briftol.
Captain Spooner.
Captain Short.

Colonel Pickering (died at Antre), now Colonel Hewfon's.
Lieutenant-Colonel Hewfon (now Colonel).
Major Jubbs (now Lieutenant-Colonel).
Captain Axtel (now Major).
Captain Hufbands (now Captain Grimes).
Captain Jenkins, flain at Farringdon, after Captain Tomkins, flain at Nafeby, now Captain Toppington.
Captain Carter.
Captain Silverwood.
Captain Gayle, flain at Briftol.
Captain Price.

Colonel Fortefcue.
Lieutenant-Colonel Richbell, flain at Taunton.
Lieutenant-Colonel Durfey, flain at Briftol.
Lieutenant-Colonel Ingoldefby, flain at Pendennis, now Lieutenant-Colonel Cobbet.
Major Jennings.
Captain Gettins, now Captain Farley.
Captain Fownes, flain at Tiverton.
Captain Young.
Captain Gollidge, flain at Taunton.
Captain Whitton.
Captain Bufhell.

[*APPENDIX.*]

Colonel Ingoldefby.
Lieutenant-Colonel Farringdon (now Lieutenant-Colonel Kelfey).
Major Cromwell, flain at Briftol, fince Major Ducket.
Captain Henry Ingoldefby.
Captain Gibfon, now Captain Stephens.
Captain Allen.
Captain Ward, flain at Briftol, fince Captain Williams, fince Captain Thomas Ingoldefby.
Captain Mills.
Captain Bamfield, now Captain Wagfhaft.
Captain Grimes.

For the Train.

Lieutenant-General Hammond, Lieutenant-General of the Ordnance.
Captain Deane, Comptroller of the Ordnance.
Mafter Hugh Peter, Chaplain to the Train.
Peter Manteau van Dalem, Engineer-General.
Captain Hooper, Engineer-Extraordinary.
Eval Tercene, Chief Engineer.
Mafter Lyon, } Engineers.
Mr Tomlinfon,
Mafter Francis Furin, Mafter Gunner of the Field.
Mafter Matthew Martin, Paymafter to the Train.

Colonel Rainfborough ([172]).
Lieutenant Colonel Bowen.
Major Done, flain at Sherborne.
Major Croffe, flain there.
Major Edwards.

---

[172] Thomas Rainborowe, murdered at Doncafter, 29 Oct. 1648, by certain Cavaliers from Pontefract Caftle. Buried at Wapping, Nov. 14. Arms, chequered or, and azure in fefs, a Moor's head in profile, bearded proper, wreathed argent.—Hunter's *Deanery of Doncafter*, vol. i. p. 26.

Captain Croffe, flain at Sherborne.
Captain Edwards.
Captain Drury.
Captain Dancer.
Captain Creamer, wounded at Sherborne.
Captain Sterne, flain at Briftol.

Colonel Welden, now Colonel Lilburne.
Lieutenant Colonel Kempfon.
Major Mafters.
Captain Peckham.
Captain Fenton.
Captain Franklin, flain at Exeter, now Captain Holmes.
Captain Dorman.
Captain Tolhuft.
Captain Munday, dead in the Weft, now Captain Welden.
Captain Kaine.
Mafter Phips, Commiffary of Ammunition.
Mr. Thomas Robinfon, Commiffary of the Draught-Horfe.

FIRELOCKS.

Captain-Lieutenant Defborough.
Captain-Lieutenant Brent.

CAPTAIN OF PIONEERS.

Captain Cheefe.

FOR THE HORSE.

Sir Thomas Fairfax, General. His troop commanded by Captain Gladman.
Major Defborough.
Captain Lawrence.
Captain Browne.
Captain Packet.
Captain Berry.

[*APPENDIX.*]

Colonel Butler.
Major Horton.
Captain Foley.
Captain Gardner.
Captain Pennyfether.
Captain Perry, dead, now Captain Bethel.

Colonel Thomas Sheffeild.
Major Fincher.
Captain Robotham.
Captain Rainſborough.
Captain Martin.
Captain Evelyn.

Colonel Fleetwood.
Major Harriſon.
Captain Coleman.
Captain Selby, ſlain at Naſeby, now Captain Laughton.
Captain Zanchy.
Captain Howard.

Colonel Roſſiter.
Major Twiſleton.
Captain Anthony Markham.
Captain Jo. Nelthrop.
Captain Peart.
Captain Henry Markham.

Lieutenant-General Cromwell.
Major Huntington.
Captain Jenkins.
Captain Middleton.
Captain John Reynolds.
Captain Buſh, ſlain at Naſeby, ſince Captain Blackwell.

Colonel Rich.
Major Alford.

Captain Nevil.
Captain Ireton.
Captain Dendy, now Captain Huſbands.
Captain Bough, now Captain Hawys.

Colonel Sir Robert Pye.
Major Tomlinſon.
Captain Margery.
Captain Knight.
Captain Barry.
Captain Rawlins.

Colonel Whaley.
Major Bethel, ſlain before Briſtol.
Captain Swallow, now Major.
Captain Groves.
Captain Cannon.
Captain Evanſon.

Colonel Graves.
Major Scroop.
Captain Flemming, Adjutant General.
Captain Lord Calfield.
Captain Bragge.
Captain Barton.

Colonel Ireton, Commiſſary General.
Major Sedaſcue.
Captain Guilliams, ſlain at Briſtol, ſince Captain Pretty.
Captain Gibbons.
Captain Hoſkins, ſlain at Naſeby, ſince Captain Cecil.
Captain Bury, now Captain Morgan.

HIS EXCELLENCY'S LIFEGUARD.

Captain Doyley, now Captain Hall.

DRAGOONS.

Colonel Okey.
Major Moore.
Captain Farmer.
Captain Mercer.
Captain Abbots.
Captain Farre.
Captain Bridge.
Captain Woggan.
Captain Skirmager.
Captain Turpin, ſince Captain Neale.

INDEX.

Abbot, —, 99
Abbots, —, 109
Abdy, Sir Christopher, 79
Acton, —, 10
Adams, Richard, 44
Addrings, Richard, 99
Adney, Clodius, 89
Aidley, —, 102
Ailworth, Walter, 34
Albany, Thomas, 31
Alcaron, Edward, 81
Aldrich, Edward, 32, 86
Alford, —, 107
Alford, William, 77
Allanby, Thomas, 68
Allen, —, 105
Allen, Edward, 43, 69
Allen, John, 67
Allen, Thomas, 67
Almot, Laurence, 46
Alured, John, 50
Alured, Lancelot, 38, 50
Alured, Matthew, 50
Anderson, Sir Henry, 51
Anderson, Isabell, 51
Andover, Lord, 6, 8
Andrew, —, 62
Andrewes, —, 39
Andrewes, Eusebius, 10
Andrewes, John, 87
Andrewes, Thomas, 88
Andrewes, William, 85
Andrews, Edward, 32, 85
Andrews, Peter, 62
Angel, —, 93
Anlaby, Sarah, 51
Anlaby, Thomas, 51
Ansell, W. 48
Anselme, William, 56

Anthony, John, 48
Apew, John, 29
Appleby, Thomas, 39
Appleton, Robert, 91
Appleyard, —, 82
Apseley, Edward, 41
Armagh, Archbishop of, 63
Armory, Edward, 75
Armstrong, —, 98
Arnett, —, 46
Arrowsmith, John, 65
Arundel, Anthony, 56
Arundel, Earl, 5
Ascough (see Ayscough)
Ash, Simon, 36
Ashburnham, Sir John, 15
Ashburnham, John, 15
Ashburnham, Wm. 15, 73
Ashcough (see Ayscough)
Ashfield, —, 102
Ashfield, John, 35, 69
Ashley, —, 62
Ashley, Bernard, 75
Ashley, Henry, 41
Ashley, Sir Jacob, 75
Ashton, Arthur, 78
Ashton, Miles, 32
Aske, —, 102
Asly, Thomas, 63
Astley, Edward, 76
Aston, Francis, 79
Atchason, James, 30
Atkins, John, 79
Atkins, Jonathan, 73
Atkins, William, 84
Atkinson, Henry, 48
Auberry, —, 81
Audey, Thomas, 83
Audley, Lord, 20

Austin, George, 54
Austin, John, 76
Axtel, —, 104
Axtell, Thomas, 43
Aysluye, Henry, 49
Ayres, Thomas, 24
Ayscough, Cecil, 67
Ayscough, Edward, 51
Ayscough, Robert, 90

Babthorpe, 10
Bacon, Robert, 85
Badger, —, 14
Baggeley, —, 96
Baggett, Henry, 83
Bagot, Richard, 68
Baildon, Cuthbert, 56
Baily, —, 66
Baily, Christopher, 31
Baily, John, 28
Baily, Thomas, 66
Bainfield, John, 70
Baker, —, 96
Baker, Robert, 40, 70
Baker, William, 50
Bakerfield, —, 95
Baldwin, John, 78
Balfoore, William, 54
Balfore, Sir William, 23
Ball, John, 56
Ballard, —, 15, 97
Ballard, Benjamin, 67
Ballard, Francis, 36
Ballard, Phillip, 32, 77
Ballard, Thomas, 43, 69, 77
Balstone, John, 28
Balyes, William, 87
Bamborough, Katherine, 51
Bamborough, Sir Wm. 51

[*INDEX.*]

Bamfeild, Joseph, 79
Bamfield, —, 105
Bamfield, John, 25
Bamfield, Sir William, 40
Bamfield, William, 70
Banard, —, 85
Banks, Chief Justice, 10
Banks, Sir John, 10
Banks, Thomas, 87
Barber, Robert, 24
Barber, Thomas, 68
Barbridge, John, 77
Barby, —, 95
Barington, Thomas, 48
Barke, William, 39
Barker, James, 30
Barker, Henry, 85
Barker, Robert, 91
Barkstead, —, 38
Barley, Phil. 55
Barne, John, 57
Barnes, Thomas, 30
Barnet, Nicholas, 89
Barnewell, Edward, 45, 70
Baron, Richard, 37
Barrell, James, 70
Barret, —, 16
Barriff, William, 46
Barriffe, Thomas, 69
Barrimore, Earl of, 78
Barry, —, 108
Barry, David, 78
Barry, Garret, 78
Barry, John, 78
Barry, Nicholas, 78
Barry, Phillip, 78
Barry, Richard, 78
Barry, Samuel, 24
Barry, William, 78
Barsey, John, 88
Barton, —, 108
Barwick, Daniel, 24
Bascarvill, —, 82
Bascarvill, Thomas, 82
Baskervill, Giles, 89
Basset, Anne, 77
Basset, Arthur, 88
Basset, Buffy, 30
Bassett, James, 80
Bateler, William, 38
Bateman, —, 17
Bates, —, 97
Bath, Earl of, 4, 8
Bathurst, Thomas, 64

Batten, William, 60
Battersby, Nicholas, 49, 55, 67
Baxter, —, 95
Baxter, Salathiel, 91
Bayles, Robert, 88
Bayley, John, 90
Bayley, Reeve, 49
Baynard, Adam, 26, 68
Baynton, Edward, 55
Baynton, James, 76
Beamont, John, 80
Beare, William, 91
Beaumont, Sir John, 80
Beckill, Robert, 48
Bedealls, Thomas, 33
Bedford, Earl of, 22, 23, 47
Bedingfeild, William, 83
Bedolph, Michael, 76
Beecher, Lionel, 82
Beecher, Oliver, 33
Beefley, —, 15
Beefton, Hugh, 36
Belasyse of Worlaby, Lord, 15
Belasyse, John, 15
Belasyse, Sir Thomas, 6
Belasyse, Thomas, 15
Belfoore, Sir William, 22
Belford, —, 93, 94
Belfore, Sir Wm. 47, 48
Bellamy, William, 89
Bellew, —, 93
Bellow, William, 84
Bellowes, William, 76
Benbriche, Robert, 89
Bendish, Roger, 89
Beneson, —, 97
Bennet, 39, 83, 95
Bennet, John, 77
Bennet, Robert, 67
Bennett, Thomas, 85
Benson, —, 93
Benson, Richard, 40, 70
Benthin, Martin, 45
Benton, —, 95
Berkenhead, —, 95
Berkshire, Earl of, 6, 8
Berry, —, 14, 106
Berry, Edward, 52
Berry, John, 85
Bertie, Montague, 5
Bertie, Robert, 4; 5, 7
Best, Thomas, 42, 86

Bethel, —, 107, 108
Betfworth, Benjamin, 41
Bettridge, Roger, 25
Betts, George, 81
Bifield, Adoniram, 39
Billiard, Thomas, 52
Billingley, —, 98
Billingfley, Henry, 39
Bingham, Celestine, 79
Bingham, Robert, 79
Bingley, Richard, 49, 70
Bird, John, 29, 50
Birke, Thomas, 89
Birkwhit, —, 96
Biron (*see* Byron)
Biscoe, —, 103
Bishop, —, 96
Bishop, Henry, 81
Blackborow, B. 53
Blackman, John, 57
Blackwell, —, 100, 107
Bladen, John, 41
Bladwell, James, 78
Blake, —, 31
Blakistone, William, 82
Blancy, —, 96
Bland, —, 102
Bland, Francis, 44
Bland, Michael, 44, 70, 87
Bland, Richard, 31, 68
Blankchard, Herbert, 69
Blansherd, —, 48
Blencarne, —, 96
Blethen, —, 103
Blewin, Peter, 32
Blith, —, 61
Blodwell, James, 36
Blount, Charles, 69
Blount, Montjoy, 5
Blowe, Robert, 30
Bluder, Henry, 87
Blundell, Henry, 41, 90
Blundell, Thomas, 41
Blunt, Charles, 29
Blunt, George, 28
Blunt, John, 75, 88
Bock, James, 29
Bodmin, Viscount, 37
Bole, Richard, 78
Boles, —, 101
Boles, Oliver, 64
Bolingbroke, Earl of, 33
Bond, Richard, 87
Bonny, Robert, 75

[INDEX.] 113

Booth, —, 92, 96
Borthvicke, —, 66
Bofa, Samuel, 49, 50
Bofome, Thomas, 86
Bough, —, 108
Boughty, William, 33
Boulton, Daniel, 78
Bourcher, William, 70
Bourchier, Henry, 4
Bowdon, —, 82 [105
Bowen, —, 5, 61, 98, 102,
Bowen, William, 26
Bower, Robert, 24
Bowerman, Henry, 86
Bowes, Toby, 91
Bowles, Robert, 79
Bowyer, Francis, 69
Bowyler, Francis, 43
Boyce, —, 102
Boyce, John, 103
Boyer, Francis, 79
Boyer, Henry, 81
Boyes, John, 77
Brach, Gervaife, 69
Bradbury, Francis, 57
Bradford, —, 96
Bradford, William, 42, 74
Bradley, Walter, 32
Bradfhaw, —, 95
Bradfhaw, Richard, 78
Bragge, —, 108
Bragge, Thomas, 85
Brakey, Jervis, 53
Bramfton, John, 32
Brand, Jafper, 32
Brand, Jofeph, 77
Brandling, Ralph, 77
Brandling, Robert, 74
Brandy, Thomas, 43
Braffe, —, 81
Bray, Edward, 91
Breckham, James, 42
Brent, —, 106
Brett, Benjamin, 83
Brett, Edward, 83
Brett, Francis, 89
Brett, Jerom, 89
Brett, Thomas, 89
Brewnett, Peter, 82
Bricknell, James, 48
Bridge, —, 109
Bridges, —, 64
Bridges, John, 29, 34
Bridges, Sir Wm. 94, 97

Bridges, William, 31, 35
Briftol, Earl of, 8, 13, 19,
Brifton, Chrift. 55 [59
Brockett, Anthony, 87
Brockett, Edmond, 80
Brockett, William, 79
Broghill, Lord, 67
Brok-haven, John, 63
Bromehall, Jofeph, 100
Brookbank, Humphry, 49
Brooke, Lord, 22, 34, 48
Broughton, Daniel, 77
Broughton, John, 31
Broughton, Robert, 81
Brown, —, 17, 93, 95, 106
Browne, Edward, 31, 68
Browne, James, 79
Browne, Sir John, 57
Browne, John, 43, 45, 53, 57, 70
Browne, Nicholas, 89
Browne, Thomas, 41, 68, 77
Browne, William, 31
Browning, Herman, 24
Brownrigge, —, 63
Broxley, Thomas, 77
Bruce, Lord, 4
Brudnell, Thomas, 49
Bruerton, —, 15
Brumley, Thomas, 87
Brufe, Robert, 50
Bryin, —, 94
Buchain, William, 57
Buck, Brutus, 85
Buckingham, Duke of, 13,
Buckley, Richard, 66 [74
Bugflock, William, 55
Bulhead, —, 17
Bunkley, —, 99
Burbeck, John, 32
Burges, Roger, 90
Burgefs, Cornelius, 27
Burgeffe, —, 64
Burgeffe, —, 66
Burgh, Chriftopher, 30, 70
Burghill, Robert, 88
Burkfley, Henry, 39
Burleigh, Jeremy, 43
Burles, William, 39
Burley, —, 18, 61
Burling, —, 96
Burrell, Bartholomew, 39
Burrell, George, 32
Burrell, James, 45

Burrell, Robert, 50
Burroughs, Jeremiah, 65
Burrowes, —, 18
Burrowes, Cafhea, 75
Burton, Humphrey, 70
Burwell, George, 88
Burwick, Lodowick, 79
Bury, —, 108
Bury, John, 38
Bury, William, 80
Burys, —, 94
Bufbridge, —, 98
Bufh, —, 107
Bufhell, —, 104
Bufhell, Anthony, 82
Bufhell, Bridges, 36
Bufhell, Thomas, 87
Butcherfield, John, 30
Butler, —, 18, 107
Butler, Francis, 70
Butler, John, 28, 81
Button, Miles, 81
Button, Thomas, 81
Byron of Rochdale, Lord, 19
Byron, John, 19
Byron, Sir John, 19
Byron, Sir Nicholas, 86
Byron, Sir Thomas, 19

Cade, Ambrofe, 40
Cadwell, —, 103
Calamy, Edward, 64
Caldecott, John, 44
Calfield, Lord, 108
Calmady, Vincent, 68
Calton, Duke, 87
Cambridge, Earl of, 3, 8
Cannon, —, 108
Cannon, Peter, 24
Cantrell, Henry, 29
Capel, Arthur, 6
Capel, Lord, 6, 9, 10, 19
Capel of Hadham, Lord, 6
Capell, William, 63
Carde, Thomas, 86
Cardinall, Thomas, 81
Carew, Edward, 33
Carew, George, 88
Carew, Henry, 31, 68
Carew, Horatio, 48, 87
Carey, Greeville, 84
Carey, Henry, 4, 5, 15, 32
Carey, Horatio, 50, 70
Carey, John, 32

Q

[INDEX.]

Carey, Sir Matthew, 88
Carey, Lucius, 9
Carleton, Thomas, 88
Carlile, Earl of, 4
Carmichaell, John, 55
Carnaby, —, 94
Carnarvon, —, 5, 8, 59
Carne, Thomas, 81
Carnoche, John, 87
Caroll, —, 64
Carr, —, 93
Carr, Ann, 31
Carr, William, 31, 83
Carrington, —, 97
Carrow, Thomas, 84
Carry (*see* Carey)
Carter, —, 97, 104
Carter, Abraham, 26, 50
Carter, John, 77
Carter, Ralf, 32
Carter, Richard, 82
Carter, William, 65
Carwardine, James, 88
Cary (*see* Carey)
Cafe, Henry, 28
Cafie, William, 33
Caffelis, Earl of, 66
Caftillion, Poynton, 84
Caftlehaven, Earl of, 20
Cafworth, —, 70
Cattarne, —, 66
Cattorill (*see* Cotterell)
Cavaler, Ifaac, 51
Cavendifh, William, 4, 5
Cawardine, Edward, 30
Cecil, 97, 108
Cecil, William, 4
Chadwell, Richard, 101
Chadwick, Lew. 56
Challys, Ifaac, 41, 81
Chaloner, Frances, 44
Chaloner, James, 44
Chaloner, Sir Thomas, 44
Chaloner, Thomas, 44
Chalwell, Phillip, 84
Chamberlain, —, 95
Chamberlain, The Lord, 7
Chambers, John, 30
Chambers, Robert, 21
Channel, Francis, 66
Chapline, Thomas, 83
Chara, —, 103
Chaune, Arthur, 77
Chayton, Henry, 74

Cheefe, —, 106
Cheney, William, 48
Chefter, —, 96
Chefter, Edward, 83
Chefterfield, Earl, 14
Cheviers, Jeremy, 82
Cheyney, William, 84
Chichefter, Ch. 55
Chichefter, Earl of, 4
Chichefter, Sir John, 16
Chichefter, Sufannah, 16
Chidley, Chriftopher, 45
Child, Francis, 101
Cholmley, Sir Henry, 38
Cholmley, Sir Hugh, 17, 38
Cholmley, Sir Richard, 38
Chonnocke, John, 87
Chrifwell, Henry, 82
Chudleigh, Chriftopher, 69
Chudley, James, 73
Church, —, 98
Churchman, Thomas, 39
Chyne, John, 82
Cicill, Benjamin, 42
Clare, Earl of, 39
Clark, George, 26
Clark, John, 102
Clarke, —, 51, 102
Clarke, Francis, 41
Clarke, Samuel, 55, 102
Clarke, William, 101
Cleare, John, 35
Clement, Thomas, 40
Cleveland, Duchefs of, 13
Clifford, Henry, 4
Clifton, John, 29, 89
Clifton, Laurence, 30
Cobb, Francis, 89
Cobb, Ifaac, 76
Cobbet, —, 102, 104
Cockaine, John, 52
Cockeram, Edward, 26
Cockin, —, 92
Codrington, Nicholas, 80
Codrington, William, 88
Cogningefby, Robert, 78
Colbie, Thomas, 76
Cole, —, 98
Cole, John, 84
Coleby, Thomas, 70
Coleman, —, 107
Coleman, Thomas, 65
Coleman, William, 35
Colesfoote, —, 17

Colield, Lambert, 87
Colle, Thomas, 63
Colledge, Thomas, 30
Collingwood, Henry, 30, 43
Collins, Digory, 89
Collins, Marmaduke, 78
Collins, Thomas, 90
Collugno, Owen, 83
Compton, Richard, 51
Compton, Spencer, 4
Compton, Thomas, 42
Comptroller, The, 9
Coney, Richard, 12
Coney, Sir Sutton, 12
Coney, Sir William, 12
Coney, William, 12
Coningham, Adam, 45
Conifby, Thomas, 90
Connant, John, 65
Conftable, Robert, 63
Conftable, Sir William, 41, [47
Conway, Edward, 74
Conway, Vifcount, 74
Coo, Thomas, 41
Cook, Francis, 66, 81
Cooke, —, 96, 101, 102
Cooke, Edward, 38
Cooke, George, 75
Cooke, Henry, 76
Cooke, Nicholas, 23
Cooke, Phillip, 78
Cooke, Richard, 86
Cooker, W. 52
Cooney, John, 77
Cooper, Coniers, 55, 67
Cooper, Marmaduke, 67
Coote, Thomas, 88
Cope, Henry, 69
Cope, William, 75
Copley, Lionel, 21
Copley, William, 21
Coquinx, Anthony, 75
Corbet, Edward, 66
Corbet, Miles, 38
Corbet, Vincent, 55
Corby, —, 30
Corey, Humphry, 87
Cornewallis, Thomas, 87
Corney, William, 87
Cornwall, Humfrey, 88
Cofbie, Arnold, 29
Cofhe, John, 51
Cofworth, —, 91
Cofworth, Samuel, 52

[*INDEX.*]

Cotsforth, Ralf, 34
Cotterell, Roger, 35
Cotterell, Thomas, 40
Cottefworth, —, 102
Cotton, —, 35
Cotton, John, 65
Couper, Marmaduke, 49
Courtney, Edward, 76
Courtney, William, 79
Courtop, —, 42
Coufe, William, 51
Coventry, Lord, 6, 9
Coventry of Aylefborough, Lord, 6
Coventry, Thomas, 6
Cowell, —, 103
Cowgrave, Francis, 83
Cowling, —, 101
Cowper, —, 96
Cox, —, 93
Cox, William, 74
Coyfhe, John, 67
Cracroft, John, 26
Crane, —, 14
Crane, John, 14
Crane, William, 67
Cratroft, John, 91
Crawford, Earl of, 19
Crawley, William, 24
Creamer, —, 106
Crelawney, —, 93
Crifp, Obadiah, 56
Crifpe, Peter, 29, 69
Crofts, Robert, 75
Croker, John, 48
Crompton, Henry, 77
Cromwell, —, 105
Cromwell, Bridget, 55
Cromwell, Elizabeth, 46
Cromwell, Sir Henry, 46
Cromwell, Margaret, 56
Cromwell, Oliver, 12, 49, 55, 56, 68, 100, 107
Crook, Samuel, 65
Crooker, Henry, 77
Cropley, Edward, 83
Croffe, —, 105, 106
Croffe, Richard, 48
Croffe, Robert, 65
Crow, Chriftopher, 45, 90
Cruttenden, Bevil, 29
Culpeper, Sir Thomas, 81
Culveer, —, 93
Cumberland, Earl of, 4, 8, 59

Cunningham, Adam, 69
Cupper, Thomas, 84
Curlys, —, 95

Dabfcoat, Thomas, 87
Daily, John, 37
Dalbier, —, 53
Dalbier, John, 23, 53
Daldorne, Henry, 55
Dallifon, Sir Charles, 36
Daliochin, James, 78
Dancer, —, 106
Dane, Michael, 39
Daniell, John, 86
Danil, Thomas, 76
Darey, —, 61
Darrenfield, —, 98
Dafhfield, —, 93
Davies, Robert, 43, 88
Davies, Thomas, 36
Davis, John, 35
Davis, Robert, 69, 88
Davis, Roland, 83
Davis, William, 81
Davifon, Alex. 54
Dawfon, Charles, 69, 86
Dawfon, Stephen, 74
Day, William, 54
Deane, —, 101, 105
Deane, Nicholas, 90
Deane, Stephen, 41
DeBoyes, Philibert Emanuel, 23, 25, 47
Deering, Edward, 32
De Fluctibus, Robert, 84
De Gennis, John, 55
Deight, —, 86
De la Blancheur, J. 55
De la Hay, John, 51
De la March, John, 66
De la Place, Samuel, 66
Dalaftey, Theodore, 80
Den, —, 94
Denbigh, Earl of, 47
Denby, —, 17
Dendy, —, 108
Denn, William, 86
Denny, Sir Edward, 69
Derby, Earl of, 5, 11
Defborough, —, 106
Dethick, William, 88
Deuolet, —, 97
Devereux, Nicholas, 26
Devereux, Robert, 20

Devonfhire, Earl of, 4, 8
Dibdale, Nicholas, 36
Dier, —, 95
Digby, George, 19
Digby, Sir John, 13
Digby, John, 8, 19
Dillingham, Thomas, 64
Dillon, —, 84, 98
Dillon, Nathaniel, 74
Dimock (*fee* Dymock)
Dingley, John, 54
Diot, —, 96
Difbrow, John, 56
Difney, —, 103
Difney, Edward, 91
Difney, Thomas, 103
Dives, Sir Lewis, 17
Dix, Humphry, 30
Dlaufherd, Herbert, 48
Dobfon, Ifaac, 29
Dobfon, Miles, 32
Dobyfon, —, 98
Dodfworth, Sir Edward, 23
Don, Daniel, 75
Done, —, 105
Doneill, —, 82
Doreflaer, Abraham, 22
Doreflaer, David, 22
Doreflaer, Ifaac, 21, 22, 47
Doreflaer, Samuel, 22
Doreflaus (*fee* Doreflaer)
Dorman, —, 106
Dormer, Robert, 5
Dorfet, Earl of, 4, 8
Dothwait, William, 69
Doughty, Mich. 88
Douglas, —, 11, 66, 93, 94
Douglas, Alexander, 48, 52
Douglas, Sir John, 88
Dover, Earl of, 5, 8, 32
Dovet, Francis, 67
Dowett, Francis, 50
Downeham, John, 53
Downes, Richard, 76
Downing, —, 65
Downing, Calybut, 37
Downing, George, 37
Dowfe, Richard. 73
Doyley, —, 108
Doyley, Sir William, 14
Drake, John, 36
Drake, Thomas, 32
Draper, Mathew, 50
Draper, Nathanael, 26

[*INDEX.*]

Draper, Thomas, 88
Draper, William, 89
Drewell, George, 83
Driver, William, 62
Drury, —, 106
Drury, Edward, 85
Ducket, —, 105
Dugdaile, John, 42
Duglafs (*fee* Douglas)
Dulbier (*fee* Dalbier)
Dungan, John, 25
Duninge, John, 64
Dunlas, George, 57
Dunfmore, Lord, 6, 9
Duppey, —, 98
Durdo, Thomas, 40
Durfey, —, 104
Dutton, Philip, 28
Dykes, —, 98
Dymmocke, Edward, 82
Dymock, —, 50
Dymock, Humphry, 32
Dymock, Thomas, 80

Ealfinan, John, 55
Earle, Walter, 53
Earnlifle, John, 78
Eafon, —, 93
Eaton, John, 77
Echlyn, Henry, 90
Edge, —, 5
Edmonds, —, 98
Edfon, Henry, 24
Edwards, —, 105, 106
Edwards, Alexander, 26
Edwards, John, 28, 74, 81
Egglefton, —, 35
Egleton, —, 97
Eldred, Benjamin, 90
Elecot, Bartholomew, 70
Elliot, Bartholomew, 45
Elliot, Elizabeth, 52
Elliot, George, 34
Elliot, Jonathan, 37
Elliot, Sir John, 52
Elliot, Richard, 76
Elliot, Thomas, 50, 55
Ellis, Meedw. 66
Ellis, Thomas, 77
Elrington, John, 87
Elfing, Chriftopher, 87
Emeley, Vifcount, 51
Emerfon, William, 31
Emmins, —, 96

Erreny, Bullen, 87
Errington, John, 91
Efline, James, 80
Effex, Charles, 45, 69
Effex, Earl of, 20, 58
Effex, Thomas, 32
Effex, Sir William, 45
Etherington, —, 9, 97
Eure, —, 103
Eure, Thomas, 41
Evans, Morgan, 100
Evans, Thomas, 55
Evanfon, —, 108
Evelyn, —, 100, 107
Evelyn, Arthur, 51
Evers, Compton, 82
Evert, William, 82
Exton, John, 87

Fairbrother, —, 98
Fairfax, Francis, 28
Fairfax, Sir Philip, 44
Fairfax, Sir Thomas, 100, 102, 106
Fairfax, Sir Wm. 43, 44
Falconberg, Vifcount, 15
Falconberg of Henknowle, Lord, 6 [6
Falconberg of Yarm, Lord,
Falconbridge, Lord, 6, 9
Falkland, Lord, 9, 59
Fane, Sir Francis, 36
Fane, Mildmay, 4
Farley, —, 104
Farley, Cuthbert, 38
Farmer, —, 109
Farnes, Jofeph, 30
Farr, Hugh, 67
Farre, —, 109
Farrew, Humfrey, 83
Farringdon, —, 105
Farrington, David, 74
Farrington, Robert, 46
Farryer, —, 11
Featly, —, 65
Feilding, Edward, 85
Feilding, Richard, 90
Fenn, —, 97
Fenton, —, 106
Fenwick, John, 42
Fenwick, Triftram, 74
Ferrer, Conftance, 70, 85
Ferrer, Conftantine, 29
Ferries, Henry, 83

Ferrors, Thomas, 88
Fidler, —, 18, 94
Fielding, —, 49, 84
Fielding, Bazil, 47
Fielding, Vifcount, 47
Fielding, William, 47
Fienes, Anne, 31
Fienes, Bridget, 31
Fienes, Conftance, 31
Fienes, Edward, 56
Fienes, Elizabeth, 31
Fienes, Francis, 53
Fienes, Henry, 53
Fienes, James, 30
Fienes, John, 31, 55
Fienes, Nathanael, 30, 52
Fienes, Richard, 31
Fienes, Sufan, 31
Fienes, William, 30
Finch, —, 83
Finch, Jonathan, 50
Fincher, —, 100, 107
Fines (*fee* Fienes)
Fifher, —, 10, 11, 96
Fifher, Henry, 44, 86
Fifher, John, 39, 89
Fifher, William, 90
Fitch, Thomas, 34
Fitfhues, Francis, 31
Fitz, Thomas, 45
Fitzgerald, John, 78
Fitz James, John, 90
Fitzmorris, —, 95
Fleetwood, —, 85, 107
Fleetwood, Charles, 10
Fleetwood, George, 10
Fleetwood, Sir William, 10
Fleetwood, William, 10
Fleming, —, 37, 100, 188
Fleming, Ch. 56
Fleming, Edward, 53
Fleming, John, 53
Fletcher, John, 87
Flexney, —, 97
Flood, —, 93
Floyd, —, 11, 92
Fludd, Katherine, 84
Fludd, Robert, 84
Fludd, Sir Thomas, 84
Flyer, —, 95
Fogge, —, 61
Foley, —, 107
Food, John, 88
Fook, Francis, 68, 69

[*INDEX.*]

Fookes, James, 37
Foord, George, 91
Forboys, Alexander, 23
Ford, —, 18
Forgifon, —, 103
Forſter, —, 18
Forteſcue, —, 102, 104
Forteſcue, Sir Faithful, 16, 28, 56, 67
Forteſcue, John, 16
Forteſcue, Thomas, 67
Foſter, —, 92
Foſter, Charles, 74
Foſter, John, 44
Fotherſby, Henry, 79
Foulkes, Francis, ſenior, 43
Fountain, Ornall, 28
Fountaine, Charles, 54
Fowke, Francis, junior, 43
Fowke, John, 24
Fowler, —, 15, 95, 97
Fowles, —, 69, 76, 84
Fowles, William, 43
Fownes, —, 104
Fox, —, 61, 93, 95
Fox, Charles, 83
Fox, John, 75, 91
Foxcroft, John, 65
Framton, William, 53
France, William, 44
Frances, —, 102
Francis, John, 39
Francis, Richard, 91
Franklin, —, 106
Franouth, Humphry, 37
Freak, John, 68
Frederick, Chriſtopher, 45
Frederick, William, 45
Freeman, —, 40
Freeman, Ralph, 87
French, —, 101
Frenchfield, —, 61
Frodſham, Edward, 25
Frodſham, Henry, 41
Froſt, —, 10
Fryer, —, 11, 95
Fuller, Chenie, 54
Fuller, George, 76
Fulwood, George, 39
Furbuſh, Thomas, 17
Furin, Francis, 105

Gage, —, 94
Gamblin, William, 88
Gamon, —, 64
Gandey, Robert, 88
Garden, George, 37
Gardiner, James, 75
Gardiner, Jer. 31
Gardiner, Thomas, 87
Gardner, —, 107
Garfeild, Henry, 91
Garfoot, William, 43, 69
Garrard, Nethermill, 41
Garret, —, 95
Garret, John, 31
Garrett, Thomas, 87
Garth, Nicholas, 38
Garth, Ralph, 40
Garts, Ralph, 70
Gates, John, 35
Gaudy, Francis, 77
Gay, Francis, 76
Gayle, —, 104
Gelaſpe, —, 66
Genings, Edward, 38
Gerard, Richard, 101
Gerrard, Charles, 76
Gerrard, Sir Gilbert, 21
Gerrard, Hugh, 80
Gettins, —, 104
Gey, —, 94
Gibb, Henry, 54
Gibbon, —, 102
Gibbons, —, 31, 108
Gibbons, Deverex, 76
Gibbons, Robert, 41
Gibbs, Higham, 75
Gibbs, Richard, 41
Gibbs, William, 89
Gibſon, —, 105
Gibſon, Richard, 81
Gibſon, Samuel, 65
Gifford, George, 44
Gifford, John, 90
Gifford, Lewis, 74
Gifford, Thomas, 87
Gilby, Theophilus, 94
Gill, William, 51
Gillmore, Charles, 83
Ginnings, Thomas, 35
Gittings, —, 30
Gladman, —, 106
Glaſcock, —, 96
Glaſſington, John, 89
Glazier, —, 96
Gleane, Peter, 85
Glenham, Henry, 11

Glenham, Sir Thomas, 11, 12, 80
Godderd, James, 49
Godfrey, Francis, 80
Godfrey, John, 89
Godfry, —, 99
Goff, —, 103
Goffe, Edmund, 75
Goldſborow, —, 29
Goldſmith, Daniel, 90
Goldſmith, David, 44
Gollidge, —, 104
Gooday, —, 102
Goodrich, John, 87
Goodrick, Daniel, 69
Goodwin, —, 39
Goodwin, Arthur, 31, 53
Goodwin, Jaſper, 36
Goodwin, Robert, 36, 82, 69
Goodwin, Thomas, 36, 64
Goodwyn, Jane, 31
Gordes, —, 102
Gordon, Nathanael, 57
Gore, Thomas, 50
Gorge, John, 42
Goring, George, 76 [19
Gothericke, Sir George, 18,
Goubourne, Thomas, 79
Gourd, Richard, 55
Gower, Stanley, 64
Grain, Robert, 41
Grandiſon, Viſcount, 13, 19, 77
Grant, Arthur, 83
Grantham, —, 47
Grantham, Francis, 41
Grantham, Thomas, 41
Gratwick, Thomas, 49
Gravenor, Edward, 34
Graves, —, 108
Graveſnor, —, 100
Gray, —, 101, 104
Gray of Grouby, Lord, 6, 29, 48
Gray of Ruthin, Lord, 6, 9
Gray of Werke, Lord, 6
Gray, Edward, 16, 29, 68, 90
Gray, Ferdinando, 29, 90
Gray, Francis, 41
Gray, Henry, 6, 29
Gray, James, 30, 42
Gray, Mathew, 90
Gray, Suſan, 6

[*INDEX.*]

Gray, Sir Thomas, 6
Gray, Thomas, 29
Gray, William, 6
Greatrix, Richard, 78
Greene, Anthony, 86
Greene, Edward, 68
Greene, John, 50, 64
Greene, Thomas, 33
Greene, William, 80
Gregson, —, 103
Grenvile, Richard, 54
Gresham, Paul, 26
Grevill, Foulke, 49
Greville, Robert, 34
Grey (*see* Gray)
Grey, Lord, 49
Griffin, —, 99
Griffin, Conyer, 85
Griffin, Thomas, 30
Griffise, —, 97
Griffith, John, 82
Griffith, Robert, 83
Grimes, —, 103, 104, 105
Grimes, James, 28
Grimes, Mark, 37, 38
Groome, Benjamin, 38
Grove, John, 87
Grover, Francis, 76
Grover, Thomas, 69
Groves, —, 108
Gualter, William, 86
Gue, Hugh, 85
Guilliams, —, 108
Gunter, John, 49
Gurney, Henry, 41
Gwalter, Thomas, 68
Gyles, —, 10

Hackluit, Edmund, 42
Hackluyt, Edward, 85
Hadon, Edmund, 54
Hakriger, —, 62
Hale, John, 54
Hale, Michael, 54
Hales, Edward, 80
Hales, Charles, 79
Halford, Nicholas, 27
Hall, —, 108
Hall, Francis, 45, 69
Hall, Henry, 66
Hamilton, Marquis of, 3,
Hamilton, —, 94 [85
Hamilton, Sir James, 87
Hamilton, James, 3

Hamlon, Robert, 88
Hammond, —, 100, 103, 105
Hamond, Edward, 90
Hamond, Francis, 90
Hamond, John, 50, 75
Hamond, Robert, 68, 90
Hamond, Thomas, 53
Hampden, John, 46
Hampden, William, 46
Hampson, George, 39
Hampson, Robert, 29
Hane, Joakim, 25
Hannam, James, 30
Harcourt, —, 42
Harcourt, Walter, 55, 91
Harcus, James, 29
Harden, —, 96
Harding, Hugh, 26
Harding, John, 56
Hardy, John, 43, 69
Harley, —, 103
Harlock, George, 39
Harris, —, 65
Harris, Leonard, 62
Harris, Nathanael, 42
Harris, Robert, 65
Harrison, —, 98, 102, 107
Harrison, James, 29
Harrow, Charles, 29
Hart, John, 40
Hartridge, George, 28, 87
Harvie, John, 33
Harvie, Robert, 42
Haselrig, Sir Arthur, 53, 64
Haselrigge, Sir Thomas, 53
Haslewood, John, 45, 76
Hastings, —, 11
Hastings, Ferdinando, 49
Hastings, Henry, 8, 11, 49
Hastings, Thomas, 26
Hatch, —, 61
Hatcher, Henry, 52, 91
Hatcher, Thomas, 56
Hatchet, —, 66
Haward, Arnold, 51
Hawkins, Leonard, 45, 69
Hawkins, Stephen, 89
Hawksworth, —, 95
Hawys, —, 108
Hay, James, 4
Haynes, Thomas, 30
Hayse, —, 93
Heaslewood, John, 88

Heath, Constantine, 101
Heithley, James, 57
Hemens, John, 29
Hemert, Walraven, 45
Hemings, —, 10
Hemings, John, 70
Hender, William, 38
Henery, Ralph, 67
Henise, Charles, 78
Herbert, —, 103
Herbert, Thomas, 101
Herbert, William, 28, 81
Herdine, John, 24
Herne, —, 97
Herne, George, 74
Herne, Robert, 80
Hertford, Marquis of, 3, 7
Hewet, William, 29, 70
Hewson, —, 104
Heyden, William, 68
Heydon, William, 31
Heyford, Anthony, 24
Heys, Walter, 37
Hickman, Thomas, 34, 49
Hickmar, Elias, 85
Hicks, John, 64
Hickson, William, 24
Hiddon, Roger, 88
Hide, David, 81
Hide, Edward, 59
Higgins, Henry, 43, 69
Higgins, Thomas, 37
Higham, George, 31
Higham, John, 79
Highfield, —, 102
Hildersham, Samuel, 66
Hilderson, John, 33, 74
Hill, —, 11, 61, 65, 95, 102
Hill, Thomas, 91
Hillyard, Sir Christopher, 14
Hillyard, Robert, 14
Hinde, Thomas, 35
Hinder, —, 103
Hinderson, —, 66
Hinton, Daniel, 35
Hippesley, Edward, 84
Hitchcock, Miles, 41
Hoare, —, 30, 96
Hoare, Thomas, 70
Hobbey, —, 11
Hodden, —, 103
Hodges, 11, 15, 18
Hodson, Benjamin, 25

[*INDEX.*]

Hodfon, John, 80
Holcroft, Charles, 31, 68
Holland, Earl of, 23
Holland, John, 83
Holles, Denzil, 39
Holles, John, 39
Hollis, John, 4
Holloway, —, 15
Holman, John, 41, 79
Holmes, —, 106
Holyday, —, 18
Holyman, Thomas, 24
Homer, —, 15
Homes, —, 96
Honey, Richard, 24
Honiburne, Lancelot, 25
Honywood, —, 92
Honywood, Philip, 76
Hooke, Benjamin, 32
Hooke, Francis, 89
Hooker, —, 94
Hooper, —, 105
Hopkinfon, John, 41
Horfey, —, 93
Horton, —, 107
Horton, Edward, 31
Horton, Jeremy, 31, 68
Horton, Thomas, 53
Hofier, —, 98
Hofkins, —, 108
Hofkins, John, 36, 75
Hotham, Sir John, 51
Houltby, Lancelot, 83
Howard of Charlton, Lord, 6, 8
Howard, —, 82, 102, 107
Howard, Charles, 6
Howard, Henry Frederick, 5
Howard, Neptune, 78
Howard, Thomas, 6, 8
Howard, William, 30
Howen, —, 99
Hoyle, —, 64
Hubbart, —, 96
Huddlefton, Henry, 89
Hudfon, Francis, 32
Hudfon, Thomas, 67
Huet, —, 15
Hugganes, Robert, 83
Hughes, John, 43
Hughes, Nicholas, 83
Hughes, Robert, 31, 68
Hulftone, Edward, 84
Hunckes, Hercules, 86

Hunfdon, Lord, 5, 32
Hunt, John, 34, 89
Hunt, Robert, 38
Hunt, Thomas, 89
Hunter, William, 37
Huntingdon, Earl of, 8, 11, 49
Huntington, —, 107
Hurry, Alexander, 37
Hurry, John, 67
Hufbands, —, 104
Hutchins, —, 96, 104, 108
Hutchinfon, —, 30
Hutchinfon, George, 70
Hutton, George, 50
Hutton, Henry, 66
Hutton, Phillip, 82
Hyde, John, 55, 68
Hyde, William, 67
Hygham, —, 97

Ingoldefby, Henry, 105
Ingoldefby, Thomas, 105
Ingoldfby, —, 95, 104, 105
Ingoldfby, Richard, 46
Innefton, —, 64
Irby, Sir Anthony, 57
Iremonger, John, 84
Ireton, —, 100, 108
Ireton, German, 55
Ireton, Henry, 55
Irwin, Mariana, 49
Irwin, Sir William, 49
Ifaac, —, 18
Ifham, Henry, 46
Ivey, John, 68

Jackfon, —, 12, 93, 95, 102
Jackfon, Edward, 74
Jackfon, John, 65
James, John, 54
Janes, Jofeph, 54
Jefford, John, 83
Jeftres, James, 74
Jellybrand, Roger, 99
Jenkins, —, 104, 107
Jenkins, Henry, 38
Jenkins, John, 45
Jennings, —, 104
Jennings, Ambrofe, 89
Jepfon, Norrice, 89
Jervas, John, 88
Jefop, John, 40
Jewks, Thomas, 49

Jewty, William, 48
Jinkins, John, 70
Jobfon, Michael, 39
Johnfon, —, 11, 17, 18, 92, 98
Johnfon, Bartholomew, 67
Johnfon, Edward, 53, 62
Johnfon, John, 26
Johnfton, Nicholas, 99
Johnftone, Sir Archibald, 66
Jolly, Richard, 49
Jones, —, 18, 92, 97, 101
Jones, Henry, 79
Jones, Humphry, 42
Jones, Richard, 38
Jordan, Elias, 62
Jordan, Jofeph, 63
Joy, Thomas, 34
Jubbs, —, 104
Jucey, William, 53
Jukes, Bartholomew, 89
Juns, Robert, 89
Juftice, Hugh, 26, 77

Kaine, —, 106
Kanyer, Francis, 79
Katcofe, Henry, 38
Keckwick, Thomas, 37
Keeling, William, 79
Keeper, The Lord, 3, 7
Kelley, —, 18
Kelly, John, 30
Kelfey, —, 103, 105
Kempfon, —, 106
Kenarick, Samuel, 44
Kent, Earl of, 6
Kent, Thomas, 77
Kerry, Lord, 68
Kettley, Thomas, 63
Kevifon, Samuel, 88
Keyes, Henry, 78
Keyghtley, Silvanus, 88
Kilmady, Vincent, 28
Kilmurrey, Lord, 16, 19
King, —, 99
King, Ralph, 83
King, Thomas, 85
Kingfton-upon-Hull, Earl of, 6, 48
Kingftone, Edward, 88
Kingftone, Thomas, 88
Kinfman, —, 82
Kirbie, Robert, 80
Kirke, Charles, 85

[*INDEX.*]

Kirke, Thomas, 76
Kirkman, —, 96
Kirle, James, 56
Kirle, Robert, 53, 56
Kirton, Pofthumus, 75
Knight, —, 108
Knight, Bray, 76
Knight, Paul, 76
Knight, William, 42
Knightly, Edward, 88
Knightly, Robert, 28
Knot, Nicholas, 90
Kowland, John, 76
Kyghley, Edward, 52

Lacey, Richard, 39
Lago, —, 103
Laham, Thomas, 29
Laighton, Harcourt, 101
Lambert, —, 103
Lambert, George, 85
Lambton, —, 94
Lamfdie, John, 43
Landen, William, 74
Lane, William, 86
Lanford, Thomas, 26
Langford, —, 30
Langford, Edward, 82
Langford, George, 41
Langham, Thomas, 81
Langhorn, Thomas, 28
Langley, —, 11
Langley, Francis, 86
Langley, John, 65
Langley, Trinity, 83
Langon, William, 76
Langrifh, Hercules, 54
Langton, Chriftopher, 35
Larrimore, Roger, 74
Latham, Thomas, 73
Latimer, Thomas, 40, 70
Laugherne, Thomas, 28
Laughton, —, 107
Laward, Thomas, 85
Lawdey, Richard, 85
Lawdy, George, 75
Lawerowyes, Ben. 77
Lawherne, Thomas, 28
Lawrence, Richard, 101
Lawrence, Thomas, 27, 39
Lawrens, —, 97, 106
Lawfon, —, 94, 97
Layton, Francis, 83
Layton, Titus, 84

Leake, George, 89
Leathcock, Humphry, 35
Lee, —, 62
Lee, Benjamin, 30
Lee, Thomas, 41
Leeds, Duke of, 18
Legard, Frances, 51
Legard, John, 51
Legg, Richard, 75
Legge, William, 15
Le Hunt, Sir John, 88
Le Hunt, Richard, 57
Leigh, —, 102
Leigh, Sir Francis, 6
Leigh, George, 79
Leigh, Goddard, 38
Leigh, Hugh, 85
Leigh, Jude, 31
Leigh, Richard, 79
Leigh, Thomas, 88
Leighton, —, 44
Leighton, Thomas, 32, 79
Lelburn (*fee* Lilburn)
Lenox, Duke of, 3, 99
Lefley, —, 97
Leventhorp, Edward, 25, 68
Lever, —, 18
Levir, —, 64
Lewens, —, 95, 96
Lewis, William, 80
Lewkner, Lewis, 81
Lewton, —, 62
Ley, —, 17
Lidcoat, Richard, 29
Lidcott, Nicholas, 82
Lidcott, Thomas, 52
Lightfoot, John, 66
Lilbourne, Robert, 5, 48
Lilburn, Edward, 35
Lilburn, John, 34
Lilburn, Richard, 34, 35
Lilburne, —. 106
Lilburne, Thomas, 35
Lile, —, 98,
Lilley, Ralph, 84
Linch, John, 42
Lindfay, Ludovick, 19
Lindfey, Earl of, 4
Lindfey, John, 53
Ling, Carax, 50
Ling, Nicholas, 35
Lion, —, 105
Lifle, Francis, 77
Lifle, George, 77, 85

Lifters —, 42
Little, George, 86
Littleton, —, 97
Llewellin, William, 44
Lloyd, —, 103
Lloyd, Broichel, 79
Lloyd, Jeffery, 32
Lloyd, John, 26, 28, 44, 81
Lloyd, Richard, 66, 77
Lloyd, Walter, 30
Lloyde, Charles, 73
Lock, Gideon, 67
Loftus, —, 98
Loftus, Samuel, 45, 70
Loftus, Thomas, 52
Long, —, 12
Long, Robert, 31, 68
Long, Walter, 55
Longueville, Lord, 6
Longueville, Charles, 6
Longueville, Sir Michael, 6
Lookar, John, 43, 69
Louch, Edward, 82
Loughborough, Lord, 11
Love-joy, Caleb, 42
Lovel, Edward, 32
Lovelace, Lord, 6, 9
Lovelace, Hugh, 88
Lovelace, John, 6
Lovell, Henry, 28, 34
Lovellis, Richard, 76
Lowe, Arthur, 83
Lowe, Laurence, 27, 74
Lower, —, 28
Lower, George, 69, 75
Lower, William, 43, 69, 76
Lowes, Phillip, 79
Lucas, —, 62
Lucas of Shenfield, Lord, 17
Lucas, Sir Charles, 17, 19
Lucas, John, 17
Lucas, Robert, 34
Luch, Ithiell, 87
Lucy, —, 17
Ludlow, Benjamin, 43
Lukine, Ifaac, 78
Lundy, —, 104
Lunsford, Henry, 84
Lunsford, Herbert, 84
Lunsford, Thomas, 84
Lunsford, Sir Thomas, 84
Luther, John, 81
Lutten, —, 60
Lutterell, John, 75

[*INDEX.*]

Lycent, John, 88
Lyng, —, 97
Lyon, Daniel, 57
Lyon, John, 23
Lyfter, Thomas, 82
Lyttelton, Sir Edward, 3
Lyttelton, Edward, 3

Maddocke, —, 93
Madox, —, 49
Madox, Da. 48
Maidftone, —, 93
Maio, —, 94
Maitland, Lord, 66
Maleroy, Avery, 82
Mallery, Robert, 29
Mallowes, Samuel, 82
Maloryc, John, 77
Malten, George, 53
Manaton, Samuel, 70
Manchefter, Earl of, 36
Mandevill, Lord, 36
Manefte, —, 102
Mangainere, Thomas, 99
Manwarring, Andrew, 69
Manwood, Jeremy, 90
March, Earl of, 3
Margery, —, 108
Marine, Robert, 57
Markham, Anthony, 107
Markham, Henry, 107
Markham, Robert, 99
Marly, John, 76
Marrow, George, 30
Marfh, —, 94
Marfh, Robert, 74
Marfhall, Anne, 27
Marfhall, Beche, 27
Marfhall, John, 34, 67, 87
Marfhall, Stephen, 27, 64
Marfhin, Henry, 77
Martaine, George, 62
Martery, Vfeus, 27
Martin, —, 107
Martin, Francis, 43, 69, 84
Martin, Matthew, 105
Marwood, James, 82
Mafham, Anthony, 31
Mafon, —, 96, 103
Mafon, Richard, 82
Maffie, Edward, 29, 68
Mafters, Geo. 82, 96, 106
Mathias, Chriftopher, 25
Matterfey, John, 35

Matthews, Henry, 90
Matthews, Simon, 48
Matthews, William, 81
Maunder, Richard, 49
Maurice, Prince, 99
May, Roger, 87
May, Thomas, 87
May, William, 81
Maylard, Edward, 85
Meautas, Philip, 69
Meldram, John, 48
Melfon, Edward, 32
Melvin, —, 104
Melvin, John, 37
Menns, Andrew, 76
Menns, Sir John, 60
Mercer, —, 109
Mercer, John, 37
Mercer, William, 67
Meredith, John, 84
Merick, Gelly, 81
Merrick, Francis, 28
Merrick, Sir John, 21, 47,
Merrick, John, 38   [81
Mefham, Thomas, 49
Metoo, —, 16
Mewe, William, 64
Mewer, Nicholas, 57
Mewer, Robert, 57
Mewer, Thomas, 57
Mewfey, —, 95
Micklethwaite, —, 64
Middleton, —, 96, 107
Middleton, John, 41, 86
Middleton, Sir Thomas, 15
Middleton, Thos. 43, 69, 88
Midehoope, I. 54
Milbourn, Mathew, 37
Mildmay, Sir Henry, 22, 54
Mildmay, Henry, 54
Mildmay, Robert, 54
Milemay, Anthony, 52
Miles, Thomas, 33
Mill, John, 37
Millar, Henry, 88
Millard, John, 77
Miller, Henry, 74
Miller, William, 42
Mills, —, 105
Mills, Francis, 83
Mills, John, 101
Milfhaw, Thomas, 81
Minn, Thomas, 79
Minfhaw, John, 40, 70

Mintridge, William, 81
Mirick (*fee* Merrick)
Mitton, —, 15
Mohun, Lord, 9
Mohun of Okehampton,
  Lord, 9
Mohun, Sir John, 9
Mohun, William, 82
Molefworth, Guy, 74
Molineux, Sir Vivian, 89
Molineux, William, 80
Mollineaux, Thomas, 89
Mollineux, Roger, 86
Molworth, Edward, 82
Momford, Peter, 43
Moncke, Arthur, 75
Moncke, George, 75
Monings, William, 43, 86
Monmouth, Earl of, 4. 8
Montague of Boughton,
  Lord, 9
Montague, Edward, 9, 36
Montague, Henry, 36
Moore, —, 94, 109
Moore, Anne, 16
Moore, Francis, 85
Moore, Gerard, 16
Moore, James, 53
Moore, Roger, 31, 68
Moore, Vifcount, 16
Moore, William, 74, 80
Mordaunt, Henry, 23
Mordent, Lewis, 34
More, —, 99
More, Daniel, 76
More, Richard, 34
Moreton, Leonard, 43, 69
Morgan, —, 13, 92, 93,
  98, 108
Morgan, Charles, 92
Morgan, James, 86
Morgan, Miles, 50, 56
Morley, —, 65
Morris, —, 46
Morris, John, 35
Morton, William, 64
Mofley, Thomas, 51
Mounfon, —, 93
Mountague, —, 103
Mountague, Lord, 9
Moufehall, —, 95
Mover, —, 62
Mowbray, Lord, 5, 8
Moyle, Nathaniel, 79

R

[*INDEX.*]

Muggridge, —, 14
Mulgrave, Earl of, 44, 49
Munday, —, 106
Munington, Richard, 87
Murrey, —, 15, 94
Murrey, Sir David, 60
Murrian, Ralph, 90
Murfchamp, Agmondifham, 69
Mufgrave, —, 14, 99
Mufhet, Fulk, 26
Mufket, —, 102
Mufon, —, 95
Mynn, Robert, 80
Mynne, John, 79
Mynne, Nicholas, 83

Napper, Sheldon, 41
Narrow, George, 70
Naffey, —, 97
Naupham, Richard, 88
Nayerne, Thomas, 69
Nayrne, Alexander, 67
Neal, Walter, 76
Neale, —, 109
Neale, Emanuel, 86
Neale, John, 50
Neale, Mofes, 42
Neale, Noah, 34
Neale, Timothy, 33
Needham, Atwell, 44
Needham, Robert, 16
Needham, Simon, 42
Needham, Vifcount, 16
Nelfon, Edward, 76
Nelfon, Robert, 70, 79
Nelthrop, John, 107
Nerne, Alexander, 57
Neve, Edward, 40
Neve, William, 80
Nevil, —, 108
Newark, Lord, 6, 9, 59
Newcaftle, Earl of, 5, 10, 48, 59
Newcomin, John, 30
Newdegate, Henry, 32
Newdegate, Richard, 49
Newport, Earl of, 5, 8, 75
Newton, John, 74
Nicholas, Edward, 9
Nicholas, Robert, 82
Nicholas, Secretary, 9, 16,
Nicholls, —, 46, 83   [59
Nicholls, Daniel, 81

Nichols, Humphry, 89
Nicholfon, —, 66
Nightingall, —, 95
Noard, Roger, 39
Noroury, Edward, 43, 69
Norcott, William, 78
Normington, Jofeph, 38
Norris, Phillip, 80
Norfhip, John, 32
Northampton, Earl of, 4
Northumberland, Earl of, 73
Norton, —, 62, 97
Norwood, Richard, 80
Noyce, } Robert, 43, 69, 76
Noyes, }
Nuby, Henry, 54
Nunney, —, 103
Nurford, Peter, 69
Nurfe, —, 98
Nye, Henry, 66
Nye, Philip, 64

Oakes, George, 91
Obrian, Henry, 78
Odingfells, Edward, 69
Ogee, William, 43
Ogle, —, 92
Ogle, Edward, 85
Ogle, Gerrard, 85
Ogle, James, 90
Ogle, Thomas, 69
Ogle, Sir William, 85
Oliver, —, 98
Okely, Edward, 25
Okey, —, 37, 38, 109
Okey, John, 48
Ondingfell, Edward, 44
O'Neill, Daniel, 18
Orfice, Richard, 28
Orpin, —, 101
Ofborne, Edward, 18
Ofborne, Richard, 70
Ofborne, Thomas, 18
Otter, Edward, 44
Otter, John, 50
Oufby, Robert, 36
Owen, —, 61, 97
Owen, Sir John, 15
Owen, John, 39
Owen, Owen, 75
Owen, Thomas, 78, 84
Owen, Walter, 81
Owen, William, 40, 81
Oxenbridge, Charles, 78

Oxenden, Richard, 91
Oxford, —, 76
Oxford, Wendy, 34

Packet, —, 106
Packington, Elizabeth, 74
Packington, Sir John, 74
Page, —, 97
Page, John, 32
Page, Sir Rife, 94
Paget, Lord, 9
Paget, William, 9
Pagett, Thomas, 83
Paholigus (*fee* Palæologus)
Paine, Jervas, 43, 86
Palæologus, Theodore, 33, 76
Palmer, —, 80
Palmer, Giles, 83
Palmer, John, 48, 89
Palmer, Peter, 53
Palmer, Robert, 36
Palmer, William, 74
Paramore, Thomas, 70, 75
Pargiter, Arthur, 42
Parin, Robert, 48
Parker, —, 98
Parker, Charles, 43, 69
Parker, Henry, 21
Parker, John, 75
Parker, Nicholas, 88
Parker, Richard, 34, 39, 82
Parkes, William, 27
Parkinfon, John, 36
Parree, —, 93
Parrimore, Thomas, 74
Parry, Owen, 31, 68, 79
Parfell, Garret, 78
Parfons, Daniel, 17
Partridge, —, 62
Pafhley, Chriftopher, 66
Pate, —, 82
Paterfon, William, 86
Patrick, William, 57
Paulet, Lord, 6, 9
Pawlet, —, 40
Pawlett, Sir John, 80
Pawlett, Thomas, 80
Pawlett, William, 80
Payard, Alexander, 40
Payne, —, 101
Payton, Sir Edward, 28
Payton, Henry, 77
Payton, Samuel, 81
Pearne, John, 67

[INDEX.] 123

Pearson, —, 97
Peart, —, 107
Peckham, —, 106
Pedar, Mathew, 56
Pemberton, Godard, 86
Pemberton, Lewis, 33
Pennyfether, —, 107
Pereont, Edward, 80
Pergent, Thomas, 86
Perren, —, 98
Perrin, —, 96
Perry, —, 107
Persall, Charles, 91
Peter, Hugh, 105
Peterborough, Earl of, 23,
Peters, Henry, 86 [28, 48
Peto, Sir Edward, 34
Peto, Henry, 86
Peto, John, 35
Pettus, Thomas, 89
Pew, Thomas, 29
Pheasant, Thomas, 78
Philips, Hugh, 39
Phillips, John, 65, 85
Phillips, Richard, 29
Philpot, —, 93
Philpot, John, 90
Phipp, Nicholas, 68
Phipps, John, 24
Phips, —, 106
Pickering, —, 104
Pickering, Benjamin, 66
Pie, Sir Robert, 55
Pierrepoint, Henry, 6
Pierrepoint, Robert, 6
Piffinch, John, 99
Pigot, Sir Thomas, 41
Pike, Henry, 90
Pilkington, Lyon, 33
Pilkinton, —, 97
Pincock, William, 30
Pindar, —, 101
Pirkins, Robert, 80
Plomer, —, 90
Plowman, Matt. 50, 56, 90
Pocklington, —, 97
Polden, —, 98
Pollard, —, 93
Pollard, Sir Hugh, 17
Polwheele, —, 93
Pomeroy, Hugh, 76, 84
Pomroy, —, 62
Poore, Francis, 87
Poore, John, 32

Pope, —, 15
Porter, —, 95, 98
Porter, Endimion, 59
Porter, Giles, 73
Potter, —, 101
Potter, Vincent, 101
Poulett, John, 6
Povey, Allen, 39, 70, 84
Powell, —, 18, 28, 84
Powell, Edward, 84
Powell, James, 88
Powell, Robert, 30
Powell, William, 83
Power, Miles, 78
Power, Richard, 85
Pownall, Henry, 42
Poyer, —, 28
Prat, —, 93
Preddocks, William, 76
Prenton, John, 86
Prestwood, —, 92
Pretty, —, 108
Pretty, Sir William, 56
Pretty, William, 49, 77
Price, —, 104
Price, Lodowicke, 78
Price, Mrs. 27
Price, Richard, 25
Price, Samuel, 40, 70
Price, Walter, 86
Pride, —, 103
Prideaux, —, 66
Prideaux, Bevil, 28
Prideaux, Prue. 30
Priest, —, 94
Primrose, —, 69
Primrose, Edward, 43
Prior, Bennet, 86
Priffe, —, 61
Pritchard, —, 98
Prowse, —, 17
Prynne, William, 34
Puckle, John, 103
Pudsey, Edward, 49
Pue, —, 94
Purpell, Robert, 43
Purpitt, Edward, 88
Purvey, Denny, 91
Pye, Sir Robert, 108
Pym, Alexander, 51

Radford, Thomas, 31
Radnor, Earl of, 37
Ragan, Cornelius, 85

Rainborowe, —, 107
Rainborowe, Thomas, 105
Rainsborough (*see* Rainborowe)
Rainsford, John, 26, 30
Ramsey, —, 93
Ramsford, John, 69
Ransom, George, 24
Rawlins, —, 76, 108
Rawlins, William, 37
Rawson, Thomas, 24
Raymant, —, 46
Raymond, John, 69
Read, —, 104
Read, John, 44
Read, Richard, 89
Redman, —, 69
Redman, Daniel, 36, 43, 87
Reed, Walter, 26
Reevs, William, 86
Reignolds, —, 65
Rewes, —, 98
Reyley, Henry, 80
Reyner, William, 63
Reynolds, John, 107
Rhodes, Sir John, 51
Rhodes, Katherine, 51
Rice, John, 28, 30
Rich, —, 10, 107
Rich, Lord, 6, 9, 19
Rich, Robert, 6
Richardson, —, 101
Richardson, Thomas, 20
Richardson, William, 88
Richbell, —, 104
Richmond, Duke of, 3, 7, 59
Ridgley, —, 15
Ridley, —, 95
Ringrose, —, 92
Rise, —, 96
Rifely, —, 94
Rifey, —, 93
Rivers, Earl, 8, 59
Robartes of Truro, Lord, 37
Robartes, John, 37
Roberts, —, 97
Roberts, Arthur, 90
Roberts, Edward, 79
Roberts, Thomas, 35
Roberts, William, 25, 34, 45, 70, 79
Robinson, Daniel, 45, 89
Robinson, Thomas, 106
Robotham, —, 107

[*INDEX.*]

Rochester, Earl of, 16
Rochford, Viscount, 32
Rocke, John, 78
Rockwood, Thomas, 87
Rodes, Sir John, 11
Roe, Henry, 25
Roe, Thomas, 42
Rogers, —, 86, 103
Rogers, Francis, 43, 91
Rogers, Thomas, 41
Rokesby (*see* Rookesby)
Rolfe, —, 103
Rolfon, William, 91
Romitree, Ralph, 51
Rooke, Ambrose, 50
Rookes, Robert, 79
Rookes, Thomas, 88
Rookesby, Anne, 51
Rookesby, Ralf, 51
Roose, —, 93
Rose, John, 36, 70
Rosington, Robert, 78
Rosley, —, 95
Ross, William, 88
Rossell, Francis, 99
Rossey, —, 95
Rossiter, —, 107
Roston, William, 79
Rotherham, George, 39
Rouse, Thomas, 38
Rowland, —, 92, 95
Rowse, George, 28, 86
Royndtree, —, 97
Rudgley, Simon, 56
Rupert [Robert], Prince, 19
Rush, Thomas, 44, 87
Rushell, Robert, 76
Rushworth, John, 101
Russell, —, 12
Russell, John, 78
Russell, William, 23
Ruston, Robert, 91
Rutherfurd, —, 66
Rutton, Thomas, 44
Ryley, —, 95

Sackville, Edward, 4
Saint John, —, 49, 76
Saint John, Sir Anthony, 25
Saint John, Barbara, 13
Saint John, Howard, 86
Saint John, Lord, 32
Saint John, Oliver, 13, 32, 68

Saint John, Sir John, 13
Saint John, John, 26
Saint Leger, William, 68
Salisbury, Earl of, 4
Salkeld, John, 74
Salmon, —, 102
Salway, Arthur, 66
Sambridge, —, 34
Samerster, Henry, 36
Sampson, —, 103
Samuel, —, 39
Sanbedge, John, 84
Sanders, —, 103
Sanders, Sir John, 56
Sanders, Mount, 32
Sanders, Pilemon, 84
Sanders, Thomas, 80
Sanderson, —, 65, 96
Sanderson, Henry, 50
Sanderson, Montague, 75
Sandes, Robert, 85
Sandford, Thomas, 74
Sands, Edwin, 48, 52
Sandys, Samuel, 74
Saunders, Edward, 52
Savage, —, 18
Savage, John, 8
Saville, Lord, 6, 9
Saville, Thomas, 6, 29
Say, Lord, 48
Say & Sele, Viscount, 30, 52
Sayer, —, 51
Scanderith, John, 82
Scarborough, Joseph, 34
Scooler, Paul, 53
Scot, —, 97
Scott, Robert, 90
Scroop, —, 108
Scrope, Adrian, 54
Scrope, Simon Thomas, 54
Scudamore, —, 82
Seaman, Lazarus, 64
Searle, Richard, 40
Sears, Joseph, 33
Sedescue, —, 67, 108
Sedgewick, Obediah, 64
Sedgwick, William, 42
Seigneur, James, 20
Selby, —, 107
Selwin, Sir Nicholas, 75
Serjeant, —, 93
Seuder, Henry, 66
Seymor, Lord, 6, 9
Seymore, Edward, 81

Seymour of Trowbridge, Lord, 6
Seymour, Francis, 6
Seymour, William, 3
Seymoure, Thomas, 85
Shafty, —, 94
Shanke, John, 39
Sharpe, —, 96
Sharpe, Francis, 50
Shawbury, Isaac, 89
Sheffeild, Thomas, 107
Sheffield of Butterwick, Lord, 44
Sheffield, Edmund, 44, 49
Sheffield, Frances, 44
Sheffield, James, 49
Sheldon, —, 13
Shelley, Henry, 69
Shelton, —, 13
Shelton, Thomas, 75, 88
Sheppard, John, 32
Sherborne, Stafford, 79
Shergall, Robert, 45
Sherley, Thomas, 86
Sherman, John, 82
Sherwood, Christian, 83
Shilling, Sheerly, 86
Shipman, Abraham, 86
Shipman, John, 45, 69, 87
Short, —, 104
Shorter, —, 46
Shute, —, 66
Sibthorpe, Henry, 77
Sidenham, —, 16
Silverwood, —, 104
Simons, —, 96
Simpson, —, 95, 97
Simpson, William, 89
Sing, Joshua, 24
Sippence, Thomas, 24
Skerrow, Robert, 84
Skinner, Thomas, 25
Skippon, —, 100, 102
Skippo*n*, Philip, 20, 21
Skipwith, Henry, 31, 68
Skipwith, John, 79
Skirmager, —, 109
Skirrough, —, 97
Skrimpshiere, John, 25
Skrimshaw, Herald, 39
Skrumshaw, Charles, 81
Skrynsheere, —, 68
Skudamore, John, 38
Skut, —, 94

[*INDEX.*] 125

Slatford, George, 41, 76
Slaughter, —, 98
Slaughter, John, 87
Sleger, Rowland, 81
Sleigh, James, 44
Slingſby, —, 60
Slingſby, Sir Henry, 17
Sloconil, Humfry, 89
Smart, —, 12
Smart, Tracey, 45
Smelomb, Barnard, 37
Smith, —, 64, 96, 98, 102,
Smith, Francis, 77   [103
Smith, Henry, 32
Smith, John, 34
Smith, Joſeph, 42
Smith, Nathaniel, 82
Smith, Nicholas, 50
Smith, Paul, 86
Smith, Richard, 86
Smith, Robert, 79
Smith, Thomas, 81
Smith, William, 60, 77
Smithwick, Francis, 80
Sneyles, —, 97
Somerſet, Duke of, 3
Someſter, Henry, 76
Sommerſton, —, 61
Song, Jenkin, 26
Southampton, Earl of, 4, 8
Southcot, —, 93
Southcot, Thomas, 38
Sowſe, —, 93
Sowton, —, 94
Spanier, James, 99
Sparkes, Ralph, 77
Sparrow, Thomas, 41
Spencer, —, 100
Spilman, Sir John, 14
Spooner, —, 104
Spooner, John, 37
Spoore, Richard, 79
Spry, William, 54
Spurflow, William, 46, 66
Stafford, —, 13
Stafforton, Thomas, 40
Stamford, Earl of, 6, 29
Stanbury, Thomas, 79
Standburgh, Humfrey, 80
Standiſh, James, 101
Standſbury, —, 60
Stane, —, 100
Stanford, —, 49
Stanhope, Ferdinando, 14

Stanhope, Philip, 14
Stanhope of Shelford, Lord, 14
Stanley, —, 11, 17
Stanley, Elizabeth, 11
Stanley, Ferdinando, 11
Stanley, James, 5
Stanley, William, 5
Stannard, William, 37
Staples, George, 67
Stapleton, Sir Philip, 26
Starkey, —, 12
Starkey, John, 30, 68
Staunton, —, 65, 93
Steed, John, 82
Stenchion, James, 57
Stephens, —, 105
Stephens, John, 62
Stepkin, Charles, 78
Sterne, —, 106
Stevens, Henry, 26
Stewart, —, 93
Stiles, —, 63
Stiles, John, 46
Stingſby, —, 61
Stoaker, Matthew, 32
Story, Francis, 87
Stradling, Francis, 87
Stradling, Henry, 63
Stradling, John, 75
Stradling, Robert, 52
Strange, Lord, 5
Strangewayes, —, 18
Stranhil, —, 101
Stratford, William, 45, 88
Stratton, —, 103
Streater, —, 102
Strelley, John, 26, 50
Strelley, Patrick, 24
Strelly, Henry, 49
Stringer, Jacob, 42, 69, 80
Stroung, Peter, 63
Strowd, —, 93
Struce, Elias, 31, 68
Stuart, James, 3
Sully, Henry, 76
Sumner, —, 42
Suſſex, Earl, 6
Sutton, —, 18
Sutton, John, 91
Swaine, William, 80
Swallow, —, 108
Swan, William, 76
Swandly, William, 62

Swanley, Charles, 61
Swanly, George, 62
Sweeper, Tho. 30
Swinford, Thomas, 90
Swright, James, 47
Symonds, Eleanor, 16
Symons, —, 96, 102

Taffe, Lord, 11
Taffe, John, 11
Taffe, Theobald, 11
Tailor (*ſee* Taylor)
Talbot, John, 90
Tapper, Nathaniel, 29
Taſburgh, Peregrine, 76
Taton, William, 35
Tayler, Henry, 34
Taylor, Francis, 64
Tempeſt, —, 95
Tempeſt, John, 13
Tempeſt, Stephen, 13
Temple, —, 66
Temple, Elizabeth, 30
Temple, James, 30, 50
Temple, John, 52
Temple, Sarah, 52
Temple, Thomas, 30, 56
Tench, —, 99
Tercene, Eval, 105
Terrill, Thomas, 54
Terwhit (*ſee* Tyrwhitt)
Tetlow, Edward, 41
Thanet, Lord, 5, 10
Thelwall, Anthony, 90
Thirlow, —, 15
Thomas, —, 17, 96, 103
Thomas, Henry, 79
Thomas, John, 63, 80
Thompſon, —, 83, 96
Thompſon, Charles, 76
Thompſon, Francis, 55
Thompſon, George, 51
Thompſon, James, 79
Thornehill, Richard, 45
Thornton, —, 82, 94
Thoroughgood,Thomas,33, 65, 86
Thorp, William, 28
Thorpe, Anthony, 81
Thory, Alexander, 29
Throckmorton, H. 41
Throckmorton, Job, 41
Throgmorton, Thomas, 76
Throughton, Iſaac, 79

[*INDEX.*]

Throwley, Edward, 54
Thurland, Richard, 81
Thwaytes, Thomas, 81
Tindall, Ambrose, 26, 70, 81
Tinne, Morgan, 30
Tinney, Morgan, 69
Tirringham, Francis, 90
Tirwhit (*see* Tyrwhitt)
Tisdale, —, 14
Tisdale, Christopher, 65
Tolhust, —, 106
Tomkins, —, 104
Tomkins, William, 78
Tomlinson, 105, 108
Tooke, James, 90
Tooley, John, 74
Toppington, —, 104
Tovey, William, 49
Townsend, Robert, 75
Townsend, Thomas, 87
Tozer, Henry, 66
Trafford, Thomas, 78
Travers, Richard, 90
Tredwell, Moses, 86
Treest, Thomas, 28
Trelawny (*see* Crelawny)
Treme, John, 28
Trenchard, John, 68
Treveere, Thomas, 11
Trevor, Daniel, 37, 87
Troughton, Christopher, 25
Trunke, William, 44
Tuchett, Mervin, 20
Tucker, —, 25, 28
Tuckey, Anthony, 65
Tufton, John, 5
Tuke, William, 86
Tukes, —, 13
Tulidaffe, Alexander, 38
Turkington, —, 36
Turner, —, 82
Turner, John, 36
Turner, Robert, 26
Turney, Isaac, 31
Turpin, —, 97, 109
Turrell, Thomas, 37
Turvill, Poole, 89
Turvill, Robert, 81
Twifield, —, 98
Twisleton, —, 107
Twist, —, 63
Tyer, —, 28
Tyerer, Edward, 90
Tyrer, Edward, 68

Tyrer, Thomas, 44
Tyrwhit, —, 96
Tyrwhit, Edward, 91
Tyrwhit, Francis, 90
Tyrwhitt, George, 44
Tyrwhitt, John, 77, 91
Tyrwhitt, Robert, 77

Udall, Sir William, 75
Ugall, Henry, 82
Upton, —, 11, 94
Upton, John, 51
Upton, Richard, 44
Urney, Edward, 77
Urrey, John, 47
Usher, George, 31
Usher, James, 78

Vahan, Sir William, 100
Valentine, Thomas, 64
Vanbraham, H. 53
Van Dalem, Peter Manteau, 105
Vanderhiden, Philip, 68
Vandowse, —, 93
Vandrusick, Jonas, 50
Vangerich, John, 67
Vanhuish, —, 93
Vanpeere, Henry, 75
Van Valkensteyn, Grijp, 22
Varnon, Thomas, 52
Vaughan, —, 98
Vaughan, Sir George, 11
Vaughan, Thomas, 75
Vaughan, Sir William, 12
Vaux, —, 18, 94
Vavasor, Sir Charles, 82
Vavasour, —, 84
Vavasour, Thomas, 14
Vavasour, Sir Walter, 14
Vavasour, William, 14, 83
Vaves, Thomas, 49
Venner, —, 11
Ventress, Charles, 88
Ventris, Henry, 85
Vernon, George, 24
Vertaine, —, 97
Vetty, Max. 54
Vicceers, —, 93
Vickerman, Ralph, 67
Villars, Edward, 77
Villiers, Anne, 74
Villiers, Barbara, 13
Villiers, Sir Edward, 13

Villiers, Sir George, 74
Villiers, George, 13, 74
Villiers, William, 13
Vincent, Edward, 91
Vines, Richard, 66
Vinkeles, R. 23
Vinter, John, 34
Vittell, John, 89
Vivers, Robert, 56
Voysey, —, 93

Waade, —, 102, 104
Wagshaft, —, 105
Wagstaff, —, 46, 70
Wagstaffe, Sir Joseph, 12
Waite, Henry, 79
Waite, John, 85
Wake, —, 61
Walbran, John Richard, 38
Walcot, Ralph, 67
Waldgrave, —, 80
Waldgrove, John, 80
Waldron, William, 82
Waldwine, —, 81
Walker, —, 62
Walker, George, 64
Walker, John, 37
Walker, Zachary, 53
Walkington, Thomas, 90
Wallen, W. 49
Waller, —, 13, 93, 95
Waller, Sir Hardress, 102
Waller, Sir Thomas, 48
Waller, Sir Wm. 40, 48, 49
Walley, —, 95
Walley, Edward, 55
Wally, Isaac, 88
Walmsley, Nath. 67
Walmsly, John, 36
Walset, Ralph, 39
Walsh, George, 32
Walter, George, 41
Walters, —, 61
Walters, John, 77
Walthall, Peter, 86
Walton, —, 90
Walton, Valentine, 56
Walwin, William, 33
Wanderford, Mi. 53
Wandlo, James, 57
Wandsford, Elizabeth, 31
Wandsford, Sir Rowland, 31
Ward, —, 63, 96, 105
Ward, Andrew, 26

[*INDEX.*] 127

Ward, Arthur, 80
Ward, Hugh, 47
Ward, Henry, 44
Ward, John, 23
Ward, Thomas, 25, 80
Wardlaw, —, 47
Wardley, William, 56
Ware, Peter, 49, 67
Warkins, John, 45
Warren, —, 77
Warren, Henry, 75
Warren, John, 35
Warren, Nicholas, 34
Warson, George, 90
Warwick, Earl of, 6, 60
Wase, Edward, 24
Wase, Roger, 45
Washer, —, 15
Washington, —, 18
Washington, Henry, 73
Washington, John, 75
Washington, Sir William, 73
Waterhouse, Joseph, 56
Waters, —, 10, 92
Waterton, —, 13
Watham, Robert, 86
Watkins, John, 70
Wats, Paul, 69
Watson, —, 100
Watson, Nicholas, 87
Watson, William, 99
Wattes, —, 61, 92
Watton, —, 56
Watton, Valentine, 56
Watts, Edward, 36, 87
Watts, John, 86
Wauton, Valentine, 56
Wayte, —, 70
Web, —, 101
Webb, James, 45, 70
Weekes, John, 75
Weekings, Luke, 30
Weeks, —, 15
Weeks, Edward, 55
Weld, John, 89
Welden, —, 106
Weller, —, 96
Wellin, William, 39
Wells, —, 92
Wells, Samuel, 45
Wentworth, George, 25
Wentworth, Henry, 79
Wentworth, William, 74
West, —, 92

West, Edmond, 55
West, Edward, 24
West, George, 54
West, Nathaniel, 50
West, William, 39
Westmorland, Earl of, 4, 8
Weston, William, 78
Wett, Edward, 43
Whaley, —, 108
Wharton, —, 49
Wharton, Lord, 31
Wharton, Philip, 31
Wheathill, Gilbert, 79
Wheeler, John, 45
Wheeler, William, 82
Wheler, —, 61
Whetstone, Roger, 36
Whife, Walter, 99
Whistler, Ralph, 49, 67
White, —, 11, 15, 92, 102
White, George, 78
White, John, 44
White, William, 29
Whiteacre, —, 11
Whitebread, John, 55
Whiteway, —, 18
Whitford, —, 94, 97
Whitford, Walter, 23
Whitgreen, —, 97
Whither, George, 80
Whitley, Matthew, 80
Whitmore, —, 97
Whitney, Francis, 90
Whitney, Thomas, 44
Whittaker, Jeremy, 65
Whitton, —, 104
Whymper, Richard, 67
Widdrington of Blankney, Lord, 17
Widdrington, Sir Wm. 17
Widnam, —, 95
Wigfal, —, 104
Wilkinson, Henry, 64
Wilkinson, Smith, 39
Wilks, —, 103
Willeby, —, 61
Willet, Edward, 46
Willey, Theophilus, 44
Williams, —, 14, 93, 105
Williams, Anthony, 86
Williams, Hugh, 79
Williams, Osborn, 36
Williams, Ralf, 45
Williams, Thomas, 25

Williams, William, 32
Willier, Francis, 86
Willis, Rawley, 40
Willis, Richard, 76
Willoughby, —, 13
Willoughby, Lord, 5, 8, 19
Willoughby de Eresby, Lord, 4, 7
Willoughby of Parham, Lord, 48, 49
Willoughby, Francis, 48
Willoughby, George, 32
Willoughby, Robert, 40
Wilmot, Henry, 16
Wilmot, Lord, 16
Wilshiere, Robert, 44
Wilson, —, 64
Wilson, Fenix, 83
Wilson, Francis, 36
Wiltshire, Robert, 77
Winchester, Alexander, 52
Wincope, Thomas, 64
Winde, —, 82
Windfeild, John, 91
Windham, George, 88
Windsor, —, 98
Windsor, Frederick, 79
Wingate, Edward, 55
Wingfield, Sir Robert, 40
Winter, —, 11, 92, 101
Winter, James, 44
Winter, William, 87
Wiseman, —, 92
Witcherly, James, 37
Witherings, Anthony, 85
Withers, —, 15
Withers, John, 45
Wivell, —, 35
Woggan, —, 109
Wolfe, —, 102
Wollaston, Sir John, 100
Wolsey, Robert, 101
Wolverstone, John, 86
Wood, John, 34
Wood, Nicholas, 36
Wood, Robert, 68
Woodhouse, —, 94
Woodman, Christopher, 91
Woodnoth, Henry, 52
Woodroffe, Foulke, 91
Woodward, John, 28
Woods, —, 81
Worsop, John, 90
Worth, Henry, 36

Wortley, Sir Francis, 12, 19
Wortley, Sir Richard, 12
Wragge, Thomas, 101
Wray, Frances, 51
Wray, Sir John, 51
Wray, Sir William, 56
Wren, John, 83
Wren, William, 27
Wright, —, 95

Wright, Gerard, 25
Wright, Samuel, 78
Wright, Vul. 79
Wriothesley, Thomas, 4
Wych, Sir Peter, 9
Wykes, —, 101
Wylde, Thomas, 74
Wynd, Robert, 77
Wynn, —, 96

Yarner, John, 42
Yate, —, 96
York, Duke of, 7
Young, —, 95, 104
Young, Arthur, 42
Young, Thomas, 65

Zanchy, —, 107

LONDON:
Printed by JOHN STRANGEWAYS, Castle St. Leicester Sq.

www.ingramcontent.com/pod-product-compliance
Lightning Source LLC
Chambersburg PA
CBHW030402100426
42812CB00028B/2804/J